Staying Sane

in

Crazy

Times

Theresa Rich, PhD

Rich Counsel Press
34067 Heritage Hills Drive
Farmington Hills, MI 48331
www.richcounsel.com
248.320.5363

ISBN 978-0-9824148-1-1

Library of Congress Control Number: 2009912841

Cover design by Joe Borri

Cover photo by Pixel

Photo of Theresa Rich by Darrell Irwin, Vivid Light Photography

For training, speaking, and consulting services based on the concepts found in *Staying Sane in Crazy Times*, please contact Theresa Rich at trich@richcounsel.com .

To my husband, Brian,

for his unwavering belief,

loving support,

and continuous encouragement.

Staying Sane
in
Cʀᴀᴢʏ Times

*Go confidently in the direction of your dreams, live the
life you've imagined.* Henry David Thoreau, Essayist,
poet & philosopher (1817 – 1862)

Introduction

The purpose of this book is to offer perspective and
tools, to help people look fear in the eye and keep
breathing, to find their opportunities, to refocus and act,
to get to the place where they want to be. To be in that
place, financially, mentally, physically, emotionally, and
spiritually, where they know and live their purpose. To not
only survive, but also to thrive in crazy times.

What we know for certain is things happen in cycles.
Times ebb and flow. Surely as winter will give way to
spring, change is inevitable. What makes the difference
is how we choose to respond and react. Will we rant at
the raging storms of winter or glory in their beauty?

For perspective, you should know this book was
written in the Detroit area during the deepest economic

crisis of nearly a century. Two of the three domestic auto companies that were the foundation of this community went through bankruptcy. Many of the businesses that rely on the industry are sinking. Portfolios are in the tank. Foreclosures are on the rise. Credit is virtually unattainable. Millions of people are out of work. The Michigan unemployment rate is 14+ percent and the national unemployment rate in double digits. The economy is stressing people out.

Whether your current craziness is due to a storm that is financial, mental, physical, emotional, spiritual or otherwise, the question now is what course you choose. Are you going to choose to let this storm rule and ruin you or are you going to choose to succeed?

This book contains stand-alone messages to help you consider where you are and what you need to do to get yourself to the place where you want to be. They are grouped based on the issues to be considered as opposed to chronologically.

At the end of every message are an assignment and two tools. The first tool is to assess where you are now and write down your personal action plan. To close out this first tool, you will be asked when you should check back with yourself to assess your progress. Put this date on your calendar. Then come back to this book on that date. Use the second tool to hold yourself accountable, to celebrate what you did do and to make a plan to address where you need to get back on course.

The idea of this book is for you to take what you need and leave what you don't. Just as our attitude is a choice, how you use this book is also a choice. For some people, it could take a year or more to work through this book. For others, it is a quick read with a bunch of feel good messages. Maybe what you need today is to read something uplifting. Great. Then what you should do for today is choose to just read and consider a message. For many people, this will give you food for thought and then you will go on with your day. If that is what you need to do today, then that is what you should do. Maybe you are ready to consider some next steps. Great. Following each message is an assignment identifying specific things to consider or actions to take. Reading through the assignment questions will encourage you to develop some generic, yet tangible, thoughts about what you can do to help take yourself to the place where you want to be. Maybe you are ready to do some action planning and move forward. Great. Taking it to an even higher level, you can use the worksheet to write your own personal action plan. By writing down your commitment you do three things: you make the action plan real; you create a way to make yourself accountable; and you give yourself a way to measure your success.

Best wishes on your journey to the place where you want to be, the place where you can be your best.

TR
December 2009

Contents

We are not permitted to choose the frame of our destiny. But what we put into it is ours. – Dag Hammarskjold, Swedish Statesman & United Nations official (1905 – 1961)

Framework

In communicating with thousands of people around the world about how crazy times affect them, I've learned a few things. First, everyone has a crazy time periodically. It may be self-imposed or occur through circumstances outside your control. However, no one has immunity from a crazy time now and again. Second, people have a mental picture deep inside of where they want to be. It is their personal place of contentment and gratitude and purpose. This is a place where they feel sane. Where they appreciate who they are and what they are contributing. Where they are making a fair number of healthy choices and are remembering to smile. For some people it means fulfilling what they believe to be God's purpose for their life. For others it is defined by their personal financial, mental, physical, emotional and spiritual measures. Third, when they are away from that place where they want to be, they are not at their best.

The purpose of this book is to help people who are in one of those crazy times and feel they are away from that place where they want to be. This book is to give those people tools to find their own way back.

From years of writing a message series that has gone to tens of thousands of people in over 20 countries, I've received a lot of feedback. Through this feedback, I've learned that there are four things that get in the way of people operating where they can be their best, in that place where they want to be. It is a progression that goes something like this:

1. They know there is a place where they want to be. Yet they are not sure of its financial, mental, physical, emotional or spiritual elements. If they do not know how to describe it, they are not likely to know if they are there. What they need is to **clarify** their vision of the place where they want to be.

2. They know where they want to be but are dealing with a loss or have fear of loss that

takes them away from that place. The separation can be financial, mental, physical, emotional, spiritual or a combination of any of these things. It leads to anxiety and emptiness. Anxiety then compounds, getting worse and worse until they are able to work through the grief cycle and deal with the loss or fear of loss. What they need is to **accept**, to look at their situation and accept that which is.

3.   They dealt with the loss/ fear of loss, but are not really sure what to pursue because there are so many possible opportunities in front of them. What they need is to **decide** how to proceed based on evaluating the possibilities.

4.   They decided which opportunities to take and which to leave; however, they have not yet done anything. What they need is to **act**, to do something.

The trapezoid on the next page shows how the progression works. We start at the top: our goal, this place where we want to be. Our personal understanding of its elements for ourselves may be anywhere along the spectrum of being very clear or very dim.

**The place where
you want to be**

Loss/Fear of Loss

Action

Choices

Opportunity

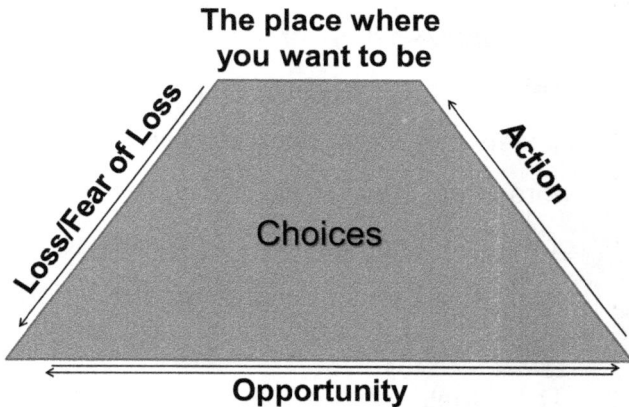

Then what happens to take us away from this
place is we experience loss or, even more commonly,
fear of loss. Like a slide down an icy slope, this loss/fear
of loss takes us away from the place where we want to
be. Once we are able to accept the situation, then we can
move on to the place of opportunity. The place of
opportunity is where we are able to consider and
evaluate possibilities. This time can be both very freeing
and very frustrating. However, to get back to the place
where you want to be, you have to take action. This could
be starting to do something positive. It could be stopping
something negative. Either way, you have to act.

In each of these stages, a person runs the risk of getting stuck forever. If a person stays stuck for too long, they run the risk of regressing backward. What moves us from one place to another is our choices.

To address this progression and help people make choices to get themselves to operating in the place where they want to be, this book is written as a series of messages and corresponding tools divided in four parts:

- Part I. **Clarify**: understanding the place where you want to be
- Part II. **Accept**: dealing with loss and fear of loss
- Part III. **Decide**: understanding and evaluating opportunities, then selecting what to do
- Part IV. **Act**: moving forward to implement your decisions

This book is written for you to use as it best suits you. Starting at Part I will not be for everyone. Start with what you need today. If your vision of the place where you want to be is cloudy, start with the messages in Part I – Clarify. If you are dealing with loss or are fearful of potential loss (for example, job loss, economic situations, health concerns, family changes), then start with the messages in Part II – Accept. If you have accepted your current situation and are feeling overwhelmed by all of the possibilities presented to you, then work through the messages in Part III – Decide. Finally, if you know what you want to do but have not yet made or implemented a plan, look to the messages in Part IV – Act.

The point is this...emotionally staying just where you are is always your choice. If you are right where you want to be, then maybe this is not the book for you. But if you are wrestling with a discontent, if you know you could be contributing at a higher level or to a higher purpose, if you feel like whatever crazy time you are experiencing is getting in the way of your higher purpose, then maybe this is the right book for you.

The choice is yours. Choose to be your best.

Clarify

PART I. Clarify: understanding the place where you want to be

Where is that place where you want to be? Your personal place of contentment and gratitude and purpose? Where you feel sane. Where you appreciate who you are and what you are contributing to your piece of the world. What mindset do you need to make a fair number of healthy choices and remember to smile?

This place is different for each of us. Some people may want to be may be living on an island, fishing during the day and dancing at night. For others, it is inventing the next great thing. For others it is raising their family or raising their health – be it financial, mental, physical, emotional or social. For some people, it may include being the boss. For others, it is helping people achieve an important vision. The key here is having a personal understanding of what is the place where you want to be – at least for today. What is that place for you?

The greatest achievement was at first and for a time a dream. The oak sleeps in the acorn; the bird waits in the egg; and in the highest vision of the soul a waking angel stirs. Dreams are the seedlings of realities. – James Allen, Author (1864-1912)

Time to bloom

The story

This morning is quite wonderful. It is still early. The sun has been up for an hour, the children will be sleeping for another two, and coffee is perking on the stove. The dog and I treat ourselves to a slightly longer walk than usual because we are simply awed by the sensory beauty of the springtime. The sky is a beautiful blue with just a hint of wispy clouds. A mild breeze floats over us. Morning sun dances on our faces. Flowering trees send out intoxicating fragrances. Birds sing greetings to each other from those trees.

When we return home, we explore our gardens. The gardens have been works in progress for our family for over 15 years. Most of the perennials are transplants from the gardens of friends or are special because we bought them during travels or to mark an anniversary. We see the yellow irises the late father of our children's first day-care provider brought up from his Kentucky birthplace. We smile when we see the striped hosta from the garden of a deceased friend who was a bonus grandmother figure for our children. Lilly of the valley from my mom's garden will soon bloom and send fragrance to the people passing the front of our home. Near the driveway are the pink and yellow tulips from the bulbs given away at another friend's wedding. Last year, they did not bloom and I was afraid they were spent. This year they are blooming again – a good omen for the couple. Wild roses and rose-of-sharon planted by birds and the breeze bud again.

On a business trip to Europe well over 10 years ago, I picked up some bulbs at the Amsterdam airport duty-free shop. Only one of the pink hyacinths still blooms, though only every two or three years. The crocuses were devoured by rabbits long ago. The tulips never did bloom.

Every year, these tulips sprouted leaves. But a flower
had yet to bloom. Until now.

Just yesterday, I noticed a red-and-yellow bloom. A
single flower. Standing up all by itself. Reaching its face
for the sunlight. After over 10 years of dormancy, now it
chooses to bloom.

The world where I live right now is beset by crazy
times economically and emotionally. Unemployment is
over 14% in Michigan and significantly higher in Detroit.
More and more people are losing their jobs. People who
have jobs are taking pay cuts and accepting demotions.
Homes are being foreclosed. Decades old businesses
are being shuttered. Bankruptcy is on the rise.

Hundreds of you have written to me to share what is
happening in your world, where you are in pain and also
how you are facing these crazy times. What is the crazy
time for you right now? Is it financial? Mental? Physical?
Emotional? Spiritual?

Here's the thing. Crazy times, crisis and pain are
going to happen. They are part of life. Out of crisis and
pain, we need to have hope and find opportunity. Now is

the time for dreams to take root. For our communities. For our companies. For our families. For ourselves.

Like my family's perennial gardens, much of what exists now was given to us by others. Some things we planted long ago. Some things we planted more recently. Some things just show up, like our wild roses. For some of us, our bulbs of reinvention were planted long ago and never flowered, like the single red-and-yellow tulip.

But maybe your time to bloom is now. Choose for this very moment to be your springtime. What is your mighty purpose? Why are you here, in this place at this time with the talents you have? Make the choice that right now you will bloom where you are planted. This very moment is your time to take any dormant or buried talents and ideas and bring them forward and nurture them into bloom.

This assignment is to dig deep into the fertile soil of your mind. Your action planning questions are these:

- What bulbs of possibility do I have – why am I here?
- Which of my talents am I holding dormant that could help?
- What will I do to get them to flower?
- Where will I use my talents to help others by nurturing the bulbs of their ideas?

Deep inside each of us are ideas just waiting to bloom. The message of my springtime garden is that now is time to do what you are on earth to do. Come up from the dirt after braving the winter and point your face toward the sun. Bring forward even your talents and ideas that have been held underground and dormant for many years. Now is your springtime. Out of the soil and the darkness, now is the time for you to bloom.

My personal action plan

What bulbs of possibility do I have – why am I here?

_____

_____

_____

_____

_____

_____

_____

_____

_____

Which of my talents am I holding dormant that could
help? _____

_____

_____

_____

_____

_____

_____

_____

What will I do to make my talents bloom?

_____
_____
_____
_____
_____
_____
_____
_____
_____

Where will I use my talents help others to bloom?

_____
_____
_____
_____
_____
_____
_____
_____

Today's Date_____

 Date I Will Check Back In _____

Being accountable to myself

What have I done to make my talents bloom?

_____

_____

_____

What do I need to do next? _____

_____

_____

_____

_____

Where have I helped someone else get their talents to bloom? _____

_____

_____

_____

What are my next steps? _____

_____

_____

_____

Date_____

This is the true joy in life, the being used for a purpose recognized by yourself as a mighty one.
– George Bernard Shaw, Winner 1925 Nobel prize for literature (1856 – 1950).

Using your 86,400 seconds for a mighty purpose

The story

Yesterday, I was honored to attend a baby shower. The mother-to-be is a young woman I have known since her early teens. She baby-sat for us when our now teenaged children were young. Now she and her husband celebrate, surrounded by loved ones, preparing to have a baby of their own.

Life milestones like these are a gift in and of themselves. In between playing silly party games, being served beautifully frosted cupcakes, and cooing over the gifts being opened, I had a chance to reflect and smile.

The road that came before this day contained joy and loss. So will the road that follows. What will make the difference is how we spend the in-between parts, the journey along the way.

Every day, we are each gifted with 86,400 seconds. How are you using that time today? Which of those seconds are you using to do no more than throw litter along your road of life, litter that could grow into great heaps of garbage keeping you from seeing what could be ahead? Which of these seconds are you using for a purpose you recognize as a mighty one?

Over the years, so many of you have written to me about your personal experiences in working to build yourself to be in the place where you want to be. You wrote about your relationships with people, organizations and communities. You wrote about your hopes and your dreams. You wrote about your personal faults and your personal failings.

Certainly I hear from some of you about your feelings concerning the litter thrown along your personal road by yourself or others. About how "some people" do not display the right behaviors. About fears. About what there is not. About what you no longer have. About events that are out of your control.

Then, there are others of you who write about how you are choosing to focus on what there is. About what you have. About what you have been gifted with. About what you can control. About contributing to a mighty purpose.

It is very easy to become consumed by our fears of what we do not have, of what is not happening, of what may be going away. We could choose to keep our focus here. It would be too bad, but it is still a choice open to us.

Or, we can choose to see what is possible and how we can contribute to getting there. Both for ourselves and for those around us. We can choose joy. We can joyfully clean up the litter around us. Yes, even in crazy times, we can choose joy.

In truth, we will each likely spend some portion of our 86,400 daily seconds on both the litter and the mighty purpose. The question for you is this: what do you choose for your balance of each? What is your plan for today?

This is assignment covers one week. It is to do a daily assessment of how you are choosing to spend your time. Where are you gifting your daily 86,400 seconds?

Which parts of your time are spent focusing on the mighty purpose of yourself or others? Are there themes around when/how/why/where you are working on getting to the place where you want to be? Do certain people help lift you in your mighty purpose?

What about when you spend your time throwing litter along your path or the paths of others? Litter piles higher and higher and will eventually block your path. Which parts of your time take away from your mighty purpose? Are there themes around when/how/why/where this happens? Do certain people only add to your litter heaps?

Finally, how much of your time should be spent attaining your mighty purpose? How do you plan to get there? What about the plans of others? How can you help?

My personal action plan

Day 1: _____% time spent on my mighty purpose; _____% time spent on litter; _____% time spent elsewhere

Observations: _____

_____

Day 2: _____% time spent on my mighty purpose; _____% time spent on litter; _____% time spent elsewhere

Observations: _____

_____

Day 3: _____% time spent on my mighty purpose; _____% time spent on litter; _____% time spent elsewhere

Observations:_____

_____

Day 4: _____% time spent on my mighty purpose; _____% time spent on litter; _____% time spent elsewhere

Observations:_____

_____

Day 5: _____% time spent on my mighty purpose; _____% time spent on litter; _____% time spent elsewhere

Observations:_____

_____

Day 6: _____% time spent on my mighty purpose; _____% time spent on litter; _____% time spent elsewhere

Observations: _____

Day 7: _____% time spent on my mighty purpose; _____% time spent on litter; _____% time spent elsewhere

Observations: _____

_____

And so, what I need to do differently:_____

_____

_____

_____

Two things I will do to make these changes:

1._____

_____

2._____

_____

This is what I want to keep the same/reinforce: _____

_____

_____

_____

_____

_____

Today's Date_____

Date I Will Check Back In _____

Being accountable to myself

What is happening with my balance right now? To what extent am I gifting my 86,400 seconds toward my mighty purpose or that of others? Place an X to show the extent to which time is spent littering, dumping trash alongside the road or contributing to a mighty purpose.

----|---|--------

Littering   Mighty Purpose

The reason for this rating is:_____

_____

_____

_____

_____

_____

These are my next steps:

1._____

_____

_____

2._____

_____

_____

Date_____

Men often become what they believe themselves to be. If I believe I cannot do something, it makes me incapable of doing it. But when I believe I can, then I acquire the ability to do it even if I didn't have it in the beginning. – Mahatma Gandhi, Political and spiritual leader of India (1869 – 1948)

Broke is a temporary condition; poor is a state of mind

The story

My college years were during what was then the worst economic time since the Great Depression. Inflation was rampant. Unemployment was high and post-college job prospects were bleak. My school friends and I were financially scraping by. We were grateful to have part-time, low-paying jobs on campus and were living from one tiny paycheck to the next. For the couple days before payday, no one would have a dollar to spare. The lack of cash would sometimes distract us from our studies.

One guy in the group would often say: "Broke is a temporary condition, poor is a state of mind." This would help remind us that we would all come through the financial drought. We would be fine as long as we kept the right perspective. We needed to focus on the greater good of achieving our education goals.

We learned to pool what we had so that all would have something. On Friday nights, a bunch of us would gather in a small apartment to have a pot-luck dinner, with everyone bringing what they had to share. What this did was allow us all to focus on what we did have, as opposed to what we did not. With a couple decades of perspective in the rear view mirror, I smile back at that time as special, filled with memories of dear friendships.

What is happening now reminds me of that time. We are in a recession. Savings have been eviscerated. Business conditions are scary. And yet....

And yet, what will make all the difference in the world is that we keep perspective. When we are in a crazy time, we need to remember to hold a positive mindset and focus on our goals. We need to turn our thoughts first to what we do have and how we can share it. Then, as necessary, turn to that which you still need.

Maybe we are broke. For some of us, that is our reality today. It could be that we are financially tapped out. Perhaps it is that we are emotionally frayed. Maybe we are spiritually teetering. Or physically we are broken. Perhaps we are weak in all four areas.

Focusing only on what we lack puts us in a nonproductive mental framework. It keeps us from believing we can achieve our purpose. Truly, if we believe we are never going to get to the place where we want to be, we won't. When we stop believing this current state is only temporary, we allow ourselves to be stuck in a place where hope dies.

At this moment, we need to accept where we are in the here and now. We need to find gratitude to celebrate that which we do have. And then we need to believe that if our current state is not the place where we want to be that this is only temporary and we can work through it. We need to choose to see opportunities.

In my recession-era college days, the place where we wanted to be meant graduating. We were all just barely scraping by, yet each of us had something to share. We had some people who could seemingly work miracles by putting together scraps of food into nourishing soups to feed our bodies and our souls. Others used their positive attitudes and their affirming words to provide strength. Still others had expertise in sports that they used to help us stay physically healthy through exercise. Working together, each of us was able to get to our place where we wanted to be.

Let's leave memory lane and move into today. What is the place where you want to be? What is that place for those around you? What do you have that you can share? And, even more importantly, how can you mutually work with others around you so you can all get to the places you want to be?

Each of us is here for a purpose. We can choose to let a crazy financial or physical or emotional or relationship or health situation distract us. Then again, we can choose something else. We can choose to use it to strengthen us and move us closer to that purpose.

Bring together the resources around you and head toward your mighty purpose, that place where you want to be. And while you do it, help others along their journey. This is the time to focus on our goals and share what we have. We may be broke, but we are not poor. Not by a long shot.

My assignment

This assignment is all about getting and sharing resources. In my recession-era college days, we were scraping by, yet each of us had something to share to make us richer as a whole. It can be the same for you.

Let's start with you. What is it that you do well? How does it help you? What do you have to spare? How can it help others?

Next, examine what it is you need to help you get to the place where you want to be. What do you already have? What do you still need that you don't have? Place each of these needs into one of these categories: financial, mental, physical, emotional, spiritual.

Finally, do a community resource analysis. What is available where you live? Search websites for your town, the local libraries, school districts, chambers of commerce. If you are into social networking, say what you need on your FaceBook or Linked-In pages.

My personal action plan

This is what I do well:_____
_____
_____
_____

Here's how it helps me:_____
_____
_____
_____

This is what I have to spare: _____
_____
_____
_____

Here's how it could help others:_____
_____
_____
_____

This is what I already have to help me get to the place
where I want to be: _____
_____
_____
_____

What I still need to get to the place where I want to be:

One financial need: _____

One mental need: _____

One physical need: _____

One emotional need: _____

One spiritual need: _____

Where I will look for what is available in my community to help me fill these needs:_____

_____

_____

What I learned is available in my community:_____

_____

_____

How I will go about asking for what I need:_____

_____

_____

_____

Today's Date_____

Date I Will Check Back In _____

Being accountable to myself

Which of my gifts am I using to help others? _____
_____

How well am I doing at this? _____
_____
_____

What could I be doing even better?_____
_____
_____
_____
_____

What do I still need to help get myself to the place where
I want to be?_____
_____
_____
_____

What is my plan to get this? _____
_____
_____
_____

Date_____

If one keeps loving faithfully what is really worth loving, and does not waste one's love on insignificant and unworthy and meaningless things, one will get more light by and by and grow stronger. – Vincent Van Gogh, Painter (1853 – 1890)

Cleaning our mental closets

The story

One positive thing I did over a recent holiday break was clean my closet. This meant taking out every single item and sorting it into four groups: keep as is, repair and keep, give away, throw away. It took hours to do. Everything in my closet is now there because it is right for me – I choose for it to there. Two huge bags of clothes were given away to a charity. A couple items went to friends or neighbors. There was a huge bagful that was thrown away. When it was over, I was filthy and tired and really glad to have tackled this task.

At the start, my closet held quite an assortment. There were things that I wear often and still like. Some things should have been discarded long ago – they may have been great for me in my 20s and are maybe not such a good idea now. There were things that were forgotten but still liked. There were things that seemed like a good idea at the time of purchase yet were hanging unused, with the tags still on them. There were things that were stained or soiled and needed to be trashed. Some things I considered dumping, but found ways to recycle into other uses. Some things were freely given to others. There were things that I received from others – either as gifts or hand-me-downs – that may still work for me, may no longer work for me, and may have never worked for me but I kept none-the-less.

As we work toward being in the place where we want to be, this experience has me thinking about our mental closets. What are the thoughts, paradigms, ideas, and habits that are hanging around in our brains? What ideals were we given or were handed down to us from others? Do they still represent our positions today? What practices seemed good once upon a time but do not work any longer? What thoughts, skills, or ideas have not been used in ages and need to be freshened up and put back into use? What is there that needs to be nurtured? What is now too big or too small?

Cleaning out my closet left me tired and dirty. Cleaning out your mental closet may be hard, tiring, and dirty work. Yet, when is it a better time to do this? If our thoughts become our words, our words become our deeds, and our deeds become our legacy, the journey to the place where you want to be is a great time to at least clear some cobwebs and know that what you keep is what you choose.

My assignment

This assignment is one that calls for looking within. What are your thoughts, habits, and practices as they relate to getting to the place where you want to be?

Some are probably spot on. Others may be more like the floppy silk ties I wore to work in the 80s – just not right in the environment today. What needs to be refreshed or renewed? What is getting in the way of your being your most effective? What are you clinging to from back in the day that no longer applies? What are the thoughts, memories and practices that should continue to be treasured, honored, and continued? What are you keeping to yourself that should be shared?

In your personal action plan, consider one of your thoughts, habits, or practices in each of these four categories:

- Keep as is
- Repair and keep
- Give away
- Throw away

My personal action plan

What is one thought, habit, or practice that supports getting me to the place where I want to be?_____

_____

_____

_____

This is what I will do to reinforce and nurture it: _____

_____

_____

_____

_____

What is one thought, habit, or practice that could help me get to the place where I want to be, but may need some repair? _____

_____

_____

_____

_____

This is what I will do to repair and nurture it:_____

_____

_____

_____

_____

_____

What is one of my thoughts, habits, or practices about the place where I want to be that could help others?

_____

_____

_____

_____

This is what I am going to do to share it with others:

_____

_____

_____

_____

What is one of my thoughts, habits, or practices about the place where I want to be that I need to abandon because it gets in the way of my success:_____

_____

_____

_____

This is what I am going to do to abandon it:_____

_____

_____

_____

_____

Today's Date_____

Date I Will Check Back In _____

Being accountable to myself

This is how I nurtured a thought, practice or habit that helps me be in the place where I want to be:

_____

_____

_____

A thought, practice, or habit that still needs repair or to be abandoned is: _____

_____

_____

_____

This is what I am going to do about it (date):_____

_____

_____

_____

_____(   )

This is where I can use one of my thoughts, practices, or habits to help someone else (date): _____

_____

_____

_____

_____(   )

Date_____

An aim in life is the only fortune worth finding. –
Robert Louis Stevenson, Essayist, poet & author (1850 –
1894)

Where you are looking is where you will go

The story

Recently, our son was granted his permit to drive.
This was a BIG DEAL to be sure. Riding in the car with
him, I was reminded of the driving lessons I've received.
There were definitely the teenaged lessons – knocking
down a neighbor's mail box when driving with my dad,
needing to call the tow truck after the "driving in reverse
in a winding school driveway" lesson with my mom, and
learning how to use a stick shift with my grandpa in an
empty parking lot.

As an adult, one memorable lesson was in a
defensive driving class a few years ago with a team of
people from work. We were learning about how to
successfully handle seemingly uncontrollable skids.

Boiled down, the lesson was "where you are looking is where you will go."

What the lesson meant was that while in a skid situation, if we focus our attention on the thing we don't want to hit, we will hit it for sure. The instructor explained that was why we so often see that cars crash center on into precisely the inanimate object that the driver wanted to avoid. Like a tree. Or a telephone pole. We learned that we should force our gaze on an open area where we want the vehicle to stop.

In sharing this lesson with our son, it made me think that this lesson is also what happens in the rest of life. Where we are looking is where we will go. If we are looking for what is wrong, we can certainly find it. Just turn on the TV or open a newspaper and you will be sure to find what is wrong. But it is not the TV or the newspaper that is the key to this. It is what we choose to gift with our attention. Take, for instance, what you choose to listen to during your commute time. Are you listening to talk radio that blasts teasers sensationalizing the news of the day? Or, are you choosing something else? Other choices include music to soothe or enthuse, comedy, sports (except in Detroit in recent years), and talk of hope and optimism.

How do you fill your thoughts in your alone time? For instance, when you brush your teeth at the end of the day, are you thinking about what you DID do or obsessing about what remains undone? When you brush your teeth in the morning are you choosing to look forward to the positive that can come from the day ahead or all the roadblocks in your way?

While it may be hard to look around the negativity and the things that didn't get done, you will be better off looking at the positive. When you are skidding, it will make the difference between feeling like you stopped in an open area from which you can drive away safely and feeling like you slammed into a tree.

Finally, if your skid is feeling out of control, get some help. Just as I needed a tow truck to get out of a ditch during the "driving in reverse on a narrow winding lane" lesson, sometimes we need help that is beyond our personal expertise.

42 | Where you are looking is where you will go

My assignment

Knowing that where you are looking is where you will go, this assignment is to start by taking a look at where you are focusing your attention. If you are choosing to look at the negative, expect the negative, and reinforce the negative, for sure your outcome will be negative.

The next part of this assignment is your "brush your teeth assignment" for the next seven days. When you brush your teeth in the morning, consider two things that you are looking forward to on that day. When you brush your teeth at night, look at yourself in the mirror and congratulate yourself for two things that you did achieve.

My personal action plan

These are positive areas where I am currently focusing my attention: _____

_____

_____

These are negative areas where I am currently focusing my attention: _____

_____

Day 1. Looking forward to:_____

_____

Achieved:_____

_____

Day 2. Looking forward to:_____

_____

Achieved:_____

_____

Day 3. Looking forward to:_____

_____

Achieved: _____

_____

Day 4. Looking forward to:_____

_____

Achieved:_____

_____

Day 5. Looking forward to:_____

_____

Achieved: _____

_____

Day 6. Looking forward to:_____

_____

Achieved: _____

_____

Day 7. Looking forward to:_____

_____

Achieved: _____

_____

My end of the week observations: _____

_____

_____

_____

_____

_____

_____

Today's Date_____

Date I Will Check Back In _____

Being accountable to myself

As I consider where I am placing my positive and negative thoughts, what do I think about the balance? Where is it consistent with getting to the place where I want to be? Where is it inconsistent? _____

_____

_____

_____

_____

_____

What do I need to choose to do to have greater emphasis on the positive items?_____

_____

_____

_____

_____

_____

_____

Date_____

You may encounter many defeats, but you must not be defeated. In fact, it may be necessary to encounter defeats, so you can know who you are, what you can rise from, how you can come out of it. – Maya Angelou, poet (1928 -   )

Comfort with falling

The story

Two summers ago, my dad had a terrible fall off a pier at night. Smashing backwards into a boat and into the water 15 feet below. The doctors told us there was little hope for him and to gather the family to say good-bye.

The doctors were proven wrong thanks to divine intervention and my dad's will to survive. The fall and ensuing months in the hospital left my dad with very little strength. They told him he'd never walk again. Then he was walking. They told him he'd never work again. The workaholic nearly lives at the office. They said he'd never drive again. And they were wrong once more.

Being in a crazy time can feel like falling backward off that dark pier. We may not have caused the crazy time to happen, but here we are in it all the same. We may not have control over when, where and how we land. We may need a lot of assistance from a lot of people to get back up.

In talking about this to my 13 year old, she informed me that she fully expects to fall down today. A bunch of times. She'll be disappointed if she doesn't. You see, she is playing in a school basketball game this evening. Her view is that if she doesn't fall, then she isn't trying hard enough.

Interesting perspective, eh? Maybe, just maybe, somewhere between my 72 year old dad and 13 year old daughter, there are lessons we need to remember. Part one is this: we WILL fall down. This is a fact of life, plain and simple. As my daughter says, if we don't fall down from time to time, we're not trying hard enough. We're not taking enough risk. Here's part two: WE CAN CHOOSE to get up. As my dad showed, getting up can take a lot of work. The difference between falling down and getting up is a lot about our choices. Sometimes we are able to get up on our own. Sometimes we need a hand from others: family, friends, loved ones, co-workers, experts. This is where we may need our community to help out.

I don't know about you, but I'm guessing we can all get a bit weary of falling down. When crazy times hit, it can sometimes feel like the best thing to do is to stay down. Sometimes that is truly the right thing for us to do. For a while. We need to figure out where we are. Why we're here. What we are learning from the situation. And then choose to get back up.

But staying down for too long means admitting defeat. Staying down is what we need to stop. To do this, we need to refocus on what is our purpose. We need to work to return to the place where we want to be, to the place of our mighty purpose, to the place where we are supposed to be. And while we're at it, we need to be sure to lend a hand to help lift up someone else.

Start today.

My assignment

This assignment is to look at your situation right now. Notice where you are falling down. Notice where are you already down and wondering what it will take to get up. Notice where you have already gotten back up. To what extent was any of this expected? What is right about your situation?

The next part of the assignment is to dispassionately look at your situation. Take it apart to see what it is that you have in your control. What do you want to change? What is your next step? What do you want to keep the same? What is your plan to keep that? Where can you anticipate falling again so that you can take some action to keep the negative impact from keeping you down? Where do you need help? If someone near you has fallen, how can you help that person get back up?

My personal action plan

Here's where I am down or falling down right now:

Expected areas:_____

_____

Unexpected areas:_____

_____

What is right about this situation is: _____

_____

_____

This is in my control:_____

_____

This is what I want to change: _____

_____

Here are two actions I will take to make these changes:

1._____

_____

2._____

_____

This is what I want to keep the same: _____

_____

_____

Here are two actions I will take to keep these things:

1._____

_____

2._____

_____

This is where I anticipate falling down again:_____

_____

I will minimize the negative impact of this next fall by

doing this:_____

_____

Where I need help from others is:_____

_____

I will get this help by doing this: _____

_____

_____

_____

Where I can help lift someone else who has fallen is to:

_____

_____

_____

Today's Date_____
Date I Will Check Back In _____

Being accountable to myself

This is how I am doing a good job at getting back up after a fall:_____

_____

_____

This is where falling still has me down: _____

_____

_____

This is how I have benefited by getting help from others:

_____

_____

This is what I need to do next:_____

_____

_____

_____

This is how I have helped lift others when they have fallen down: _____

_____

_____

These are my next steps:

    1._____

    2._____

Date_____

Accept

PART II. Accept: dealing with loss and fear of loss

Loss and fear of loss take us away from the place where we want to be. Like a rat making wood shavings out of a perfectly good piece of furniture, we gnaw away at ourselves and our psyches. Our emotions become more and more frayed, shredded into a rat's nest. We fight admitting where we are and moving on to do something about it. Instead, we churn and churn and churn. We become trapped like a rat, unable to move forward. The slide down the slippery slope of fear and loss continues until we accept where we are and choose to do something about it.

Failure to accept our current situation places us deeper in loss. We choose to become victims. We choose to have the emotional rats gnawing away at our confidence, propelling us further downward and instigating greater fear and anxiety and emptiness. Until we are able to go through the process of grieving that we are not where we want to be, we will not be able to move forward to be there. Once you have acceptance, you can have hope. And then you can move forward to the place where you want to be.

Empty pockets never held anyone back. Only empty heads and empty hearts can do that. – Norman Vincent Peale, Clergyman & author (1898 – 1993)

Running on empty

The story

How do you refuel when your tank is empty? Not in your vehicle. I'm talking about your internal tank, the reservoir that keeps you up and moving, engaged and productive.

Sometimes, our internal tanks are close to empty. The "low fuel" light is on and we're just about running on fumes. We all feel that way sometimes, I think. We can feel empty because of running too hard on things both good and bad. I typically feel this way at the end of a major project or life event.

What causes this varies from person to person. Sometimes it can be because of too much work. Big projects. Crazy deadlines. Travel. Sometimes it can be because of too much family drama – life changes for happy things, life changes that may be sad. Day to day with kids, spouses, parents, in-laws, neighbors, friends. Maybe we are physically hurting, or sick, or just tired. Even vacations can be exhausting. We may also see people behaving toward us in ways that display the personal stress they are feeling. Then we choose to let the lowered fuel level of others drain us.

Experiencing personal "low fuel" warnings impacts us immensely. We get mentally and sometimes physically weary. Our patience grows short and our tempers flare more easily. We can feel spiritually lost.

Sometimes we choose to respond to low fuel warnings by backing away. This can result in isolation. Sometimes we choose to respond to low fuel warnings by frenetic activity. And when our energy is spent, we are again alone and with even less fuel than when we started.

It is good to know in advance how to identify when our own personal "low fuel" light is about to go on and know how to find alternative fuel sources. Do you know your personal warning signs? Are you short tempered? Easily irritated? Do you have trouble sleeping? Isolate yourself from friends and activities you previously enjoyed?

What is important is to recognize that what may refuel one person may not refuel another. For some people, being around too many people causes the fuel to run low. And then it is through introspective, quiet time that refueling occurs. For others, the solitude that may come with a crazy time like job loss causes the energy to run dry. Then it may be time to find a career transition networking group or engage in a reasonable amount of social networking to reconnect.

The thing to remember is the quote from Norman Vincent Peale at the start of this chapter. No matter what thing or things you may lack at this moment, where to focus is on what you do have. Right here. Right now. It is only when we allow ourselves to believe we have nothing do we get to the point where we choose to turn our attention to making that true.

What it is you may need today is the time to focus on what you do have. What are the things in your control? If your current crazy time is due to finances, it could be that your pockets are empty. Maybe they are not empty but it is the fear of empty pockets that has you stressed. This does not take away from the character of who you are. Some of the greatest success stories are people who went through bad economic patches. So it can be for you.

As you go through this crazy time, remember to preserve your dignity and that of the people around you. Having a bad day (or month or year) is not a valid excuse for bad behavior. Watch your temper. Mind your tongue. Speak kindly. Remember that every person in your line of contact also has his or her own crazy things that may cause the low fuel warning to be lit. Choose to practice compassion for yourself and those around you.

My assignment

This assignment is to consider two questions.

First, what causes your fuel to run low? By knowing what causes you to run on empty, you can try to avoid these things or at least prepare yourself to notice and anticipate that they are occurring. Consider what choices you have other than to just run dry.

Second, what are your alternative fuel sources? This refers to what you can do to refuel your body, mind, and spirit. Maybe it is exercise, prayer, alone time, music, reading, volunteering, being surrounded by others. By having your strategy in advance, you won't be caught on empty with no fuel source in sight.

My personal action plan

These things cause my fuel to run out: _____

_____

_____

_____

_____

_____

_____

They typically happen when I am:_____

_____

_____

_____

_____

These are my warning signals that my fuel is running low:

_____

_____

_____

_____

_____

_____

_____

_____

_____

These are the things that refuel me: _____

_____

_____

_____

_____

_____

_____

This is what I can do to make sure I always have
sufficient fuel: _____

_____

_____

_____

_____

_____

_____

_____

_____

_____

_____

_____

Today's Date_____
Date I Will Check Back In _____

Being accountable to myself

Where is my fuel level today? Do I have sufficient stores or am I again (still) running low?

---|---|---

Empty   Full

What is my plan to refuel? _____

_____

_____

_____

What is my plan to keep your tank filled? _____

_____

_____

_____

How am I doing at practicing compassion for myself and those around me? _____

_____

_____

What is my next step? _____

_____

_____

_____

Date_____

A pessimist sees the difficulty in every opportunity; an optimist sees the opportunity in every difficulty. –
Winston Churchill, British prime minister, statesman, and author (1874 – 1965)

Handling a series of unfortunate events

The story

When our kids were younger, we treasured reading stories together at bedtime. One series they loved in their late elementary years was *A Series of Unfortunate Events* by Lemony Snicket. The series begins with three children spending a happy day at the beach when they are told their parents died in a fire that destroyed their home. Throughout the 13 books, the children's hopes are repeatedly dashed by the devious Count Olaf who seeks to inherit their family fortune.   Each of the children has a talent. Violet (about 12) is creative and invents things. Klaus (about 10) is a voracious reader and has great book knowledge. Sunny (a baby) has three sharp teeth and likes to bite. Despite the evil schemes of Count

Olaf and his minions, the orphans get themselves out of every situation by combining their talents.

The lessons of these books are helpful to us as we work through crazy times. On the one hand, things may feel dreadful. We may be nervous, apprehensive, afraid. Crazy times bring great uncertainty. If not you, then perhaps those are the feelings of others around you.

But here's the thing. We – each of us – have that thing that we do well, that job that is ours to achieve, that role that is ours to play. Like the baby that has only three sharp teeth, you may feel like that thing you have and do is small. No matter. When each of us stays focused on what we can do, as opposed to the things we cannot control; when we combine our small and large talents together, as opposed to fretting over what we cannot do; when we keep a positive outlook, as opposed to looking at what is bad … it is then that we achieve greatness. It is then that there is promise and hope.

No matter how crazy things may be for you in this moment, there is still a lot that is in your control. First, you can choose to take a clear-eyed view of what is happening right now. Not in a way that judges what is good or bad – just in a way to acknowledge what is.

Second, you can choose to accept that the thing most in your control is how you decide to respond. Finally, you can choose to see what resources you bring to improve the situation. Even if you are like the baby who has only her three sharp teeth and a willingness to bite, there is still goodness and help and relief you can choose to bring into this crazy time.

My assignment

This assignment is to stay focused and help others to do the same. There is plenty out there to distract us. Yet worrying about that will not make these crazy times any better. What you can do is choose to take on a leadership role – whether at home, at work or in your community. Be visible. Ask people how they are doing. Truly listen to what they have to say. And then help them refocus on doing their best every day. If people around you are hurting, help them up.

For yourself, do your best to tune out the distractions. Make healthy choices. Have gratitude for the talents you have and then use them to your fullest every day. Like the orphans in the stories, the best way through crazy times is to appreciate and combine our collective talents.

Finally, consider where you may have latent talents. In crazy times, we sometimes have the freedom of creativity. There is no better time to try something new and different. It just may help.

My personal action plan

These are people I need to ask how they are doing. This will allow me to listen and learn how I can best support their getting through this crazy time and to the place where they want to be:_____

_____

_____

_____

Because one conversation does not a relationship make and because things change – especially in crazy times – this is my plan to periodically check back in with them:

1._____

_____

2._____

_____

3._____

_____

These are my talents that may help get me and others through this crazy time: _____

_____

_____

_____

Here are some ways my talents can be used:

1._____

_____

2._____

_____

These are the talents of others that may help get me through this crazy time: _____

_____

_____

Here are some ways those talents can be combined with mine and those of others:

1._____

_____

2._____

_____

Here are some opportunities to grow some talents that may not have been developed in the past:

1._____

_____

2._____

_____

Today's Date_____

Date I Will Check Back In _____

Being accountable to myself

This is what I have learned from my conversations with others on how these crazy times are affecting them:

_____

_____

_____

This is what I still would like to understand:_____

_____

Here is my plan to gain this understanding:_____

_____

This is how I am better using my talents and those of others:_____

_____

This is what I need to do next:_____

_____

These are the new talents I am trying out:_____

_____

_____

These are my next steps: _____

_____

_____

Date_____

You cannot always control what goes on outside. But you can always control what goes on inside. – Wayne Dyer, Author & speaker (1940 –   )

Dealing with a flooded engine

With our son driving now, long forgotten driving memories come back to the front of my mind. My first car was a medium blue six year old Plymouth Duster. Imagine my surprise coming to our home and seeing it with the red big bow my parents placed on the top. Like most of my early vehicles, it turned well over 130,000 miles before I moved on to something else. And being a new teenaged driver, I worked that car hard.

One memory about that car is that it was fussy. It went from zero to 60 if and when it felt like it. As these were the days long before fuel injection, I flooded the engine pretty regularly. For those who have not experienced a flooded engine, to my non-engineer brain that means I gave the engine too much gas and I wasn't going to be able to get the car to start until it rested a bit. No amount of stomping my feet, yelling at the car, or pouting would get that car to start any faster than it felt like starting. So I learned to take a breath and wait.

I think the same thing happens to us. Sometimes, our personal engines get flooded. There is so much that comes at us that we need to just stop and rest a bit before we can start back up.

Recently, I had one of those rare, wonderful evenings where everything was perfect. The weather was lovely. Spring was clearly on its way. It was a good day at work. We had a healthy, home-cooked dinner as a family. Dinner dishes were done. Our kids were outside playing ball in the waning daylight. I was in my pajamas watching a little TV with my husband and puppy before going to bed to be ready for yet another 6 a.m. meeting the next day. All was right with the world.

Then the phone rang. It was a dear friend who was just leaving work (three hours after I was already home). She said "come meet me at the Starbucks." So I got dressed and went out to meet her. She's dealing with her husband preparing for cancer treatment, yet another round of impending job reductions at work, large pay cuts coming for those remaining with the company, one child waiting to hear back from college applications, elder parent health matters, out-of-town siblings who increase the anxiety level every time they make a well-intentioned call to find out what's going on, an upcoming family vacation, and minimal personal time to build her own resilience. The conversation is summed up by her statement "I never thought I would say that dealing with my husband's cancer would be the least of my stressors."

Like the engine on my first car, my friend's engine was flooded big time that night. The good news is that she knew how to handle it. She needed to take a breath and rest her engine a bit. So we sat in the Starbucks and laughed over our lattes until our tears flowed. Once she had given herself a break to breathe, she was ready to move forward. She kept perspective and didn't let potential stressors so bombard her psyche that she lost focus. Instead, she wisely focused on what was in her control.

In all of our lives, there are potential stressors aplenty. Commercials designed to make you think not having one particular type of health insurance carrier or a doctor from a specific hospital affiliation could cause you to die. Headlines blaring messages of negativity and dire consequences. Double digit jobless rates and increasing foreclosures. Knowing that fear sells, TV news programs hook you into viewing because watching that one particular program could save you from ruin, your marriage from destruction, your children from predators, your family from catastrophe, your job from elimination. All that is missing from some of these ads is that watching will save your soul from eternal damnation.

For my friend at the Starbucks, what she cannot control is a lot. And yet, what she can control is also a lot. Most specifically, she can choose her attitude. She can refrain from obsessing about what is outside of her control, like the progression of her mom's recently diagnosed memory loss. She can avoid sliding down the slope of negative what-if future scenarios. She understands what issues are important, like her husband's cancer, and is also calmed by looking at facts and culling out sensational headlines.

There are a number of realities that can be learned from this situation. First, each of us experiences a flooded engine from time to time. Things outside of our control bombard us constantly. If we let ourselves, we could have a constantly flooded engine. The challenge, then, is in the balance. How to make sure we have enough fuel to help us do what we need to do while at the same time stopping the flow of fuel before the engine floods. Second, we have control over our response. We can choose to increase or decrease the extent to which we have negative messages in our environment. We can choose to respond in ways that are uplifting and promote self-health.

What does this mean? Before you move any further away from that place where you can be your best for today, you need to stop. Breathe. Focusing on what you cannot control will only increase your stress level. Rather than let the stressors send you down a slippery slope away from being your best, look at your choices. You can choose to let your engine flood by all that is bombarding you. Or, you can choose to focus on what you can control and strive to handle that well. Truly, that choice is yours.

My assignment

This assignment is to first write down the things that are bombarding you and keeping you from being the best you can be today. What is a healthy, personal way for you to sort through what is and is not in your control? Next, write down which of these things are within your control. It is only by focusing on the things within your control that you will be able to keep your engine from flooding. And it is only by keeping your engine from flooding that you will be able to be at your personal best.

Once you know what is in your control, then is the time for action planning. What specific actions can you take – starting today? When will you get to the other items?

My personal action plan

What is flooding my engine right now?_____

_____

_____

_____

_____

_____

_____

_____

_____

_____

What is a healthy way to sort what is in my control?

_____

_____

_____

_____

_____

_____

_____

_____

_____

_____

What specific actions can I take today?

_____

_____

_____

_____

_____

_____

_____

What will I do to address the other items in my control?

_____

_____

_____

_____

_____

_____

_____

_____

_____

_____

Today's Date_____

Date I Will Check Back In _____

Being accountable to myself

What actions did I take to deal with my crazy time in a
healthy way? _____

_____

_____

What went well with what I tried? Why?_____

_____

_____

What did not go so well? Why? _____

_____

_____

_____

What's my next step? _____

_____

_____

_____

_____

_____

_____

Date_____

Remember, if you ever need a helping hand, it's at the end of your arm. As you get older, remember you have another hand: The first is to help yourself, the second is to help others. – Audrey Hepburn, Actor & humanitarian (1919 – 1993)

Making sure your air mask is in place

The story

The first email I opened at the start of one week was from a friend asking me to write a message he could use with his organization that was going through a hard time. His people were stressed. People were losing jobs all around them. Burned out. Hopeless. Afraid. Looking between the lines, my friend was also having a personal crisis. He was trying to lead others while going through trauma himself. Could this email have been written by you? Are you going through a crazy time? Is fear keeping you from being mentally, physically, emotionally, and financially in the place where you want to be? Are you finding yourself in such a care-taking role that you are missing out on taking care of yourself?

In trying to do well in our many roles, we sometimes find that we are giving and giving and giving. And then we find that we have nothing left for ourselves. When we take that moment of private time, we figure out that we have the same doubts and fears as the people around us. When our spouse or our children or our neighbors or our team members ask "will we be okay?" the truth is that they are only giving voice to the same questions we have inside our heads.

While no one wants to hear it in the middle of a crazy time, it is the crazy times that shape our character and push us to achieve more than we may have thought possible. Think about the achievements of which you are most proud. Were they because of something handed to you or were they the product of crazy times? Think about the people you most trust. Chances are that you went through the test of crazy times together and now know you can rely on each other.

If we are wise, we recognize that it is during crazy times that we also find opportunity. This is the time we are willing to consider taking risks. This is the time we are ready to be creative. This is the time we are able to say "why not" and embrace reinvention, renewal, and rebirth.

When the crazy times come, the first thing to do is make sure you stay healthy and whole – mind, body, spirit. Get enough sleep. Exercise. Be grateful. Eat right. Pray. Meditate. Pray. Breathe. Smile. Laugh. Practice gratitude. Be optimistic. Achieve something every day.

The journey to the place where you want to be will likely take a long time. You need to make sure you are packed and ready for the trip. Once you ensure your self-sanity, you are better able to help others. It is like making sure your air mask works on an airplane before helping the person sitting next to you. You cannot help someone else if you cannot breathe.

This assignment starts with making sure you are putting on your air mask first. What healthy habits are you embracing? Where would you like to do even more? Where are you embracing unhealthy habits or finding comfort in things that feel good in the moment, yet you know are not good for you? What is your plan to cut back on the unhealthy habits you are embracing?

By calling out what is happening and giving it a name, you will be better equipped to stop any potential or additional slide away from being your best. It is easy to point at others and observe how badly they are doing. However, it is only by taking care of oneself first that we are able to help others and, at the same time, ourselves.

My personal action plan

What am I doing to take care of myself first? _____

_____

_____

_____

_____

Where am I embracing healthy habits? _____

_____

_____

_____

_____

Where am I making choices that could be more healthy?

_____

_____

_____

_____

_____

_____

Where would I like to improve even more? _____

_____

_____

_____

_____

_____

_____

Where am I embracing unhealthy habits? _____

_____

_____

_____

What is my plan to add more healthy choices/cut back on the unhealthy choices? _____

_____

_____

_____

_____

_____

_____

_____

Today's Date_____
Date I Will Check Back In _____

Being accountable to myself

Where am I putting on my air mask first? _____
_____
_____

Where am I trying to take care of others to my own
detriment? _____
_____
_____
_____

What two changes should I put in place?

1. _____
   _____

2. _____
   _____

What is my plan to make these two things happen?

_____
_____
_____
_____
_____
_____

Date_____

It is not the strongest who survives, but the one who is able to adapt. – Charles Darwin, Naturalist (1809 – 1882)

The two sniffing dogs test

During crazy times, it is important to keep our resilience stores well stocked. Resilience is what allows us to be better able adapt, come what may.

A tricky thing about building resilience is finding something that works for you. Sure, we all know the basics about making healthy choices: eat right, exercise, sleep, spend time with friends/family. But when it comes to specific choices, what builds one person's resilience could also sap another's.

Knowing the difference is important. In our family, we use the "two dogs sniffing each other" test. It comes from one of my dad's many sayings. If one of us invites Dad to go somewhere or do something that does not interest him, he says "I'd rather watch two dogs sniffing each other." Now perhaps others may say "no thank you." However, my dad's phrase makes it crystal clear where his interests do and do not lie. What it shows is his clarity about what does build his resilience (the things he wants to do) and the things that do not (hence, his phrase).

In early 2009, I sent out a request to my readers to share what they are doing to build resilience. Some of these things may seem like good ideas for you. For others, you may find watching two sniffing dogs more restorative than the suggested activity. Knowing the difference for you is what is most important.

Here are some of the reader suggestions:

- At age 50+, I'm taking figure skating classes. When I share this, I find other people sharing with me their "out of the comfort zone" activities. I met a woman who started playing soccer in her mid-40's, and marathon runners and ballroom dancers of all ages!
- I volunteer coach a sports program for special needs kids. It puts a lot of other things in perspective.
- I've discovered on-line social networking and re-discovered a bunch of school friends on FaceBook.
- I cook and have people come over to eat. What started as a way to be creative is now a social outlet.

- My thing is knitting. I enjoy figuring out patterns and then seeing how they come out.
- I LOVE the old *I Love Lucy* re-runs. No matter how my day went, after a Lucy show, I'm smiling again.
- With the weather about to turn warm, I look forward to being in the garden with my hands in the soil, the sun on my face, and potential in my heart.
- Coming home to a dog that is happy to see me and a cat that couldn't care less helps me know both that I am loved and to not take myself too seriously.
- Once a day I go to a high floor in this building and look out over beauty of Seoul. Once a month I go for a hike in the mountains.
- Here's a new exercise I'm trying: every day I take a look in the mirror and find five things that are good about me. By the end of the week, I have a mental list of 35 positive things about myself.
- I joined Weight Watchers. Now I'm down 15 pounds!
- I solve puzzles: sudoku, crosswords, word search.
- I hit the road on my Harley.

As you read, there was a wide variety of suggestions. Perhaps some of these resilience builders appeal to you as something that could help fuel your soul. Quite probably, some of these resilience builders seem as helpful and appealing as watching the two sniffing dogs. Regardless, what we know for sure is that life is messy and crazy times come. What helps us survive effectively is having a store of resilience and a way to keep that store well filled. Resilience reserves will help you keep perspective and see what is positive.

My assignment

This assignment is to consider your personal resilience stores. First, what drains your resilience? Where are you the poster child of "what not to do?" Which of these things can you release so as to not do further damage to your psyche?

Next, when you finish reading this paragraph, close your eyes, take a deep breath, and smile. Before you open your eyes, keep smiling and take ten slow breaths, letting your shoulders relax and allowing your mind to calm. Complete this sentence: *what makes me strong is* _____. Close your eyes and begin now.

What did you see? Start there. What you saw in these moments are things that can calm and build you. Whatever it is that was captured in that moment is where you need to start.

Finally, give back. What can you do to equip others? To help others build their resilience?

My personal action plan

This is what drains my resilience:_____

_____

_____

_____

_____

_____

When I close my eyes, breathe deeply and smile, these
are two things I see:

1._____

_____

_____

_____

_____

2._____

_____

_____

_____

_____

How do these things make me stronger?_____

_____

_____

_____

_____

A way I can do more of what makes me stronger is
to:_____

_____

_____

_____

I commit to doing this for myself by:_____

_____

_____

_____

_____

_____

_____

A specific person I can help build the resilience of is:

_____

I will help equip this person in building his/her own
resilience by doing this: _____

_____

_____

_____

_____

Today's Date_____
Date I Will Check Back In _____

Being accountable to myself

What have I done to implement my action plan for
myself?_____

_____

On a scale of 1-10, where do I rate my personal
resilience today?

```
---|-------------------------|------------------------------|-----
   1                         5                             10
  Low                     Medium                         High
```

If I rated myself lower than where I want to be, what do I
plan to do about it? _____

_____

_____

_____

How am I doing at equipping someone else in building
their personal resilience? _____

_____

_____

_____

Date_____

After every storm the sun will smile; for every problem there is a solution, and the soul's indefeasible duty is to be of good cheer. – William R. Alger, Minister & author (1822 – 1905)

The little dog and the storm

The story

We have a little dog. He's not much of a dog. He's mostly fur and bark. Somewhere in his 8 pounds, he packs in a ton of alpha dog attitude. His best trick is shedding black fur when I'm wearing white and white fur when I'm wearing black.

Like many little dogs, he fearlessly rules the household and spends his days barking at squirrels who dare to scamper into his line of sight. He totally owns the heart of everyone in our family.

On a recent Friday night, we experienced a raging rainstorm. The dog hates storms. They scare him witless. The storm started rolling in a bit after midnight. We knew it because the dog started pacing throughout the house, his nails clicking on the wood floors. By 3 a.m., the storm was howling and so was the dog. The poor little thing was moaning and crying. He was on our bed. Off our bed. On our bed. Off our bed. On our bed, pawing insistently until I would get up with him. He knew for sure he wasn't happy. He wasn't sure what he wanted to do about it. But he was certain he wanted me there with him.

Rather than let him wake the rest of the household, I got up with the dog and went into another part of the house. We paced for a while. Then we went outside – yes, in the pounding rain at 3 a.m. – then we went back inside. Then we went outside again. And inside again. He was totally freaked out by the storm and could not be consoled. Finally exhausted by lack of sleep and the dog's anxiety, I fell asleep on the sofa and quit noticing when he would jump on and off of me.

When daylight came, the storm was beyond us. The dog was calmly nestled at my feet at the end of the sofa.

So what are the lessons from the little dog and the storm? One thing is that no matter how tough and strong we may feel when times are good, everyone is scared by something. Sometimes we can work it out by pacing and thinking and planning. Considering options. Looking at possibilities. Sometimes, we need to let loose and howl. We need to let others know what we are thinking and feeling. Sometimes, we need to seek out company and consolation from people we trust. Sometimes, we need to check out other options – outside and inside. Exploring options can feel like going outside into a driving rain at 3 a.m., with the wind whipping around you and lightning striking. Yet that may be exactly the right thing to do at the time. Sometimes we need to go somewhere else.

Does a crazy time have a storm raging within you right now? If so, you probably don't like it. Maybe it feels scary. You may not know how long it is going to last. You may not know when daylight will come. Sometimes it can feel as though the warm, sunny light of day may never return. Yet return it will.

While we certainly can't be ready for everything, we have some advantages over the dog. What we can do is be prepared. We can look at the spectrum of things that can happen during the storm of a crazy time and plan for what we will do. Unlike the little dog that is acting on instinct and seeing the storm as only bad, we can look for the opportunities that can come from times of change. We can choose to examine the horizon and see the possibilities. We can choose to have hope. To believe in ourselves. To build our resilience. To help others who are having a more difficult time. To smile in the knowledge that storms pass and new days do dawn.

My assignment

This assignment is to take a personal inventory. Where are your strengths that can help you through the storm of a crazy time? If you are in the storm of a crazy time right now, what are the opportunities of this particular storm? Where does this give you the opening to take on new challenges? To consider possibilities? To test yourself? Are others in this storm with you? Where can you help others get through the storm of this crazy time?

If you are feeling overwhelmed and need to howl at the storm, go ahead and do it. If you need help from others, be sure to get it. Then when you're done howling, move on.

My personal action plan

This is a listing of my personal assets that can help me through whatever the storm of this crazy time may bring:

Financial:_____

_____

_____

Mental:_____

_____

_____

Physical:_____

_____

_____

Emotional:_____

_____

_____

Spiritual:_____

_____

_____

If I am in a storm today, these are ways I can use my personal inventory to help myself through it:

_____

_____

_____

_____

_____

_____

_____

_____

Who else is going through this storm?_____

_____

_____

These are ways I can use my personal assets to help others through this economic storm: _____

_____

_____

_____

_____

_____

Today's Date_____

Date I Will Check Back In _____

Being accountable to myself

How am I using my personal assets to get through my
current storm? _____

_____

_____

_____

_____

What would help me even more?_____

_____

_____

_____

What is my plan to obtain this?_____

_____

_____

_____

How am I helping someone else?_____

_____

_____

_____

Date_____

Decide

PART III. Decide: understanding and evaluating opportunities, then selecting what to do

As we move from loss and fear, we transition to a place of hope and opportunity. This is a place of possibility…and EVERYTHING is possible. This is also a place where we can get stuck in the tar and never really move on to the place where we want to be. Effectively using our time here is highly important. It is also important to resist sliding back into fear of more loss.

At this phase, the opportunities can be overwhelming. Do you want to become an astronaut or take a nap? Do you want to walk around the block or write an epic novel? Like the kid in front of the candy counter, the risk is to be so overwhelmed by the possibilities that we never choose. Yet, not to decide is to decide. What it means is we decide to stay stuck and never make it to the place where we want to be.

And so, until the time comes that we decide, we remain stuck. We even risk regressing back to the place of fear and loss.

If you are earnest, if you truly want to move forward to the place where you want to be, you must choose a path. You must decide what you will do to move forward and make peace within yourself of what you are leaving behind.

Take advantage of the ambiguity in the world. Look at something and think what else it might be.
Roger von Oech – Internationally recognized leader in stimulating creativity and innovation

Ambiguity Avenue

The story

In the US, this past weekend's Labor Day national holiday marks the unofficial end of summer. The sun rises later and sets earlier. Kids return to school. Leaves on the trees take on their autumn hues.

For many people, this time of year is a time of personal introspection. What is happening with my life? Where am I proud? Where have I been less than my best self? What is next? It is also a time to examine the company we keep and those from whom we became separated this past year. Who were the people who were beside us when we accomplished great things? Who were the people who sharpened our thoughts by challenging us? Who softened disappointment by supporting us? Who must we let go of?

And now, we look at what is next. Whether we are remaining in our current life situation or moving on to something else, we all live on Ambiguity Avenue. Anxiety and fear live on the dark and shadowy side of this street. Calm and hope live on the other. The question is this: which side of Ambiguity Avenue will we choose to gift with our time?

It is very easy to seek solace on the shadowy side of Ambiguity Avenue. We can be lured there by concerns of the unknown. We can allow ourselves to be overcome. If we stay where we are, there are questions. How will staying where I am help me achieve my purpose and become my best possible self? How will staying where I am stand in the way of moving to the place where I want to be? What if I'm not yet up to becoming my best possible self? Whom can I trust?

If we move on – whether by choice or otherwise, there are questions. Now what do I do? What does this do to my personal identity? What does this mean for my image in the eyes of others? Do I care? What does change mean for me financially? What is the impact on my family and loved ones? What happens to my work/social network? To whom do I have to explain my choices? How do I make those explanations?

Yet Ambiguity Avenue has a sunny side. A place of calm and hope and possibility and opportunity. It is also yours to choose. This does not mean you should ignore the dark and shadowy questions. For without one side, how can there be another? By all means, ask and answer the questions for yourself. It is just that you can choose to not dwell there.

It is within your control to spend more time on the sunny side of Ambiguity Avenue. The best way to do this is to build your personal resilience. Make healthy choices. Exercise. Eat right. Lay off the alcohol. Spend time with your loved ones. Turn toward your higher power. Get your sleep. Encourage others. Turn off the 24/7 news networks that stay alive by hyping all that is bad in the world. Listen to uplifting music. Look at what is right with your situation. Consider what may be other possibilities. Network. Breathe.

This assignment starts with introspection. What ambiguity are you facing today? To what extent are you on the dark and shadowy side of Ambiguity Avenue? To what extent are you in the sunshine?

Next, look to your personal resilience. What each of us knows for sure is we have had crazy times before. We will each of us have them again. The key to getting to the place where you want to be is in your personal resilience.

What are three commitments you can make with and to yourself to build your resilience? Make one commitment to yourself that is physical. Make one commitment to yourself that is mental. Make one commitment to yourself that is emotional/ spiritual.

Finally, be personally accountable to yourself. Consider sharing your commitments with someone else. Sharing makes them more real and helps you be more likely to succeed because you know someone else is there to lend a helping hand.

My personal action plan

The level of ambiguity in my life today is:

--|--------------------------------|--------------------------------|----

Low   Medium   High

The reason for this rating is:

_____

_____

_____

_____

_____

_____

While on Ambiguity Avenue, I am spending my efforts:

----------|--|---------

On the shadowy side   On the sunny side

Here are examples to illustrate this rating:

1.:_____

_____

2._____

_____

3._____

_____

My commitments to build my resilience are:

1. Physical commitment:_____

_____

_____

2. Mental commitment: _____

_____

_____

3. Emotional/spiritual commitment: _____

_____

_____

This is how I am going to make sure I stay personally accountable to myself for building my resilience and being able to spend more of my effort on the sunny side of Ambiguity Avenue: _____

_____

_____

_____

_____

_____

_____

Today's Date_____

Date I Will Check Back In _____

Being accountable to myself

How am I doing on my three commitments to build my resilience?

1.Physical commitment:_____
_____
_____

2. Mental commitment: _____
_____
_____

3. Emotional/spiritual commitment: _____
_____

How has building my resilience affected how I am spending my time on Ambiguity Avenue? Am I spending more or less time on the sunny side? On the shadowy side?_____
_____
_____

What's my next step? _____
_____

Date_____

It is no good getting furious if you get stuck. What I do is keep thinking about the problem but work on something else. Sometimes it is years before I see the way forward. In the case of information loss and black holes, it was 29 years – Stephen Hawking, Theoretical physicist & author (1942 -   )

Finishing your flip

The story

On a trip to the Florida Keys, my husband and I went parasailing. I loved flying high in the sky with the colorful parachute above me, seeing the sun sparkle on the water below. When the boat below me sped up, I'd soar back into the sky. When it slowed down, I'd float to the water. When the boat driver suggested that I do a flip in the air, I was game. When I was way up high in the air I started the flip – got halfway through the somersault – then I froze. Right there in the air. I got scared. My head was pointed down toward the water, my feet and backside were in the air. My arms twisted above me. Despite the warm Florida sun, my hands were frozen in a grip on the harness, unwilling to let go.

This is what sometimes happens with us during transitions. Even for good things. We get to the point where it is time to let go of what was and we get stuck. When have you felt like that? The feeling of "yes, I would really like to _____ (fill in the blank with the thing you want to do), and I do not because _____" gets in the way of all of us from time to time.

The question to ask yourself is this: what is the rest of the sentence, the part after the "because _____." What goes in the rest of the sentence is your rationalization. It can be something you fear. It can just be something unknown. We freeze when we do not finish the sentence, to say "...and I do not because _____ (fill in the blank with your response)".

The short while I was hanging upside down in the air, with the harness uncomfortably pressing my breakfast against my gut, I had the chance to fill in the rest of my sentence. I did not allow myself to let go of the ropes because I was afraid I would fall. In thinking it through, the thing I was afraid of was silly. I was not going to fall. I was in a harness and the parachute was holding me up. I let go and finished the flip.

By filling in the blank, you give a name to what keeps you stuck. You now have something to deal with. You can start the conversation within your head or with others about what to do next. When we look back at the times we were unable to let go and then finally did, sometimes we find that the thing that was mentally stopping us was not rational. Sometimes the thing in our way is big and needs to be confronted. By identifying the thing that has you frozen, you can decide for yourself whether it truly should leave you frozen or whether it is something you can handle.

So now you are dealing with a crazy time. Maybe it is financial, mental, physical, emotional, and/or spiritual. You feel like you are upside down and falling, with an ache in your gut that has you nauseous. You are hanging there, frozen, not sure what to do next. Unable to move.

No doubt about it, crazy times are hard. They test us. They seem to torture us. And yet. And yet it is in precisely the crazy times that we need to pause. Assess the situation. Take a breath. If we are scared, allow ourselves some time to be afraid. If we have to cry, then we need to allow ourselves to cry. And then…. Then it is time to deal with the crazy time. It is time to take that deep breath and move forward.

My assignment

This assignment is to notice where you are stuck today. Start by giving it a name. Then move on to identify what is happening with it. Not in a way that is judging, just in a way where you can look at it, nod your head and say "yes, this is what is happening."

Are there times when you are more or less stuck than other times? Notice when this happens. Are there any themes or trends around these times? What are they? Are there times when you are more creative and flowing than others? When is that? Are there times in your control? What are the themes there?

Finally, consider why you are allowing yourself to stay stuck. Are you stuck because this is where you need to be right now? If so, work on something else until it is the right time to address this particular issue. However, if it is time to move on, consider the possibilities of what could happen if you let go from this place of stuckness.

My personal action plan

This is what has me stuck today:_____

_____

It has elements that are (check all that apply):

_____ Financial

_____ Mental

_____ Physical

_____ Emotional

_____ Spiritual

This is how it is pulling me from the place where I want to
be/fulfilling my mighty purpose:_____

_____

_____

I have been choosing to let it keep me stuck because:

_____

_____

These are the times when I am less stuck than other
times:_____

_____

These are the times when I am more stuck than other
times:_____

_____

Is it time to move on from this place of stuckness?

_____ Yes   _____ No

Why? _____

_____

_____

_____

This is what I need to do to let go of this thing that has

me stuck: _____

_____

_____

_____

Here are the next three action steps to let go of the thing

keeping me stuck (and date when I plan to take these

steps):

1. _____

_____(_____)

2. _____

_____(_____)

3. _____

_____(_____)

Today's Date_____

Date I Will Check Back In _____

Being accountable to myself

How am I doing at letting go of the thing keeping me
stuck?_____

_____

_____

What am I still choosing to hold on to? _____

_____

_____

Why?_____

_____

_____

_____

What is my next step? _____

_____

_____

_____

_____

_____

_____

Date_____

An unexamined life is not worth living. – Socrates, Greek philosopher (469- 399 BC)

Course correction

Ever lost your way? It happened to me one beautiful Saturday. I was taking our dog to a groomer that is located less than five minutes away from our home. Fifteen minutes later, with music playing on the radio and a warm breeze from the open sunroof tossing my hair, the dog and I were still in the car moving down the road and we were nowhere near the groomer.

Losing our way happens to us all. Sometimes, it is something small – like our trip to the groomer. Sometimes, it is something larger. Airline pilots say flying a plane requires continuous course correction. This course correction is done with an objective realization that action needs to be taken and then taking it. It is not done with remorse or self-recrimination. It is just done with matter-of-fact acceptance that it needs to be done. So it should be for us.

If we truly are off course, now is a good time to acknowledge it and course correct – without remorse or self-recrimination. Now is also a great time to celebrate where we are on course and where our course has found us. Finally, now is a great time to provide ourselves some feedback.

The point is this. We each of us lose our way for periods long and short. Certainly there are a zillion reasons this can happen. Sometimes it is because we are just going merrily along (or maybe just going along, without the "merrily" part). Sometimes inertia has us in place and we just keep doing what we have been doing because it is our routine. Sometimes we are where we are because of something that seemed to be a good idea at the time. We get stuck in the rut of our day to day life and no longer remember how to get out. And that place where we want to be becomes a dim light in the dark recesses of our psyche.

It is easy to come up with excuses for why we are no longer striving to get to that place where we want to be. If your craziness is financial, you can talk about how credit is tight and jobs are scarce. After all. After all. After all.

Choose today to stop the excuses. Choose today to return your focus to that place where you want to be, to your place of purpose. Turn the page and to do a compass check. Take another look at that place where you think you want to be. See where it still fits you and you still fit it. Celebrate where you are on target. Write down – without judging – which adjustments need to be made. Remember that course correction is natural and appropriate. Choose to make those course corrections and get back on track.

My assignment

This assignment is to examine where your life is now. Take a breath, reflect, and give yourself some feedback. Whether intentionally or inadvertently, are you on the right course?

What is about perfect the course you are traveling today? Why have you found this path? Why did this path find you? Where you are on course, write down what you are doing to reinforce your positive results. What can you do to stay open to new possibilities?

Are you off course completely? Write down three things you can do to course correct so you can get back on your way. Once you have your three course corrections, write down your plan to make them.

My personal action plan

Where is the place I want to be? _____

_____

_____

_____

Am I there or headed there?

_____Yes _____No _____ Not sure

Explain_____

_____

_____

In what ways am I on this course intentionally or
inadvertently? _____

_____

_____

_____

_____

What is perfect about where I am today? _____

_____

_____

_____

_____

How can I reinforce what I am doing well today?

_____

_____

_____

_____

Where am I off course?_____

_____

_____

_____

What three things will I do to course correct?

1._____

_____

_____

2._____

_____

_____

3._____

_____

_____

Today's Date_____

Date I Will Check Back In _____

Being accountable to myself

How's my personal action plan going?

------|---|-----
   On target   Off target

Where have I made course correction that should be
celebrated? _____

_____

_____

What course correction do I still need? _____

_____

_____

How can I make this situation even better?_____

_____

_____

How can I help someone else with their course
correction? _____

_____

_____

What's my personal next step?_____

_____

_____

_____

Date_____

Far better it is to dare mighty things, to win glorious triumphs, even though checkered by failure, than to take rank with the poor spirits who neither enjoy much nor suffer much, because they live in the gray twilight that knows not victory nor defeat. – Theodore Roosevelt, US president (1858 – 1919)

Making transitions

The story

Transitions of all forms happen to each of us all of the time. Happy changes. Sad changes. Work changes. Family changes. Physical changes. Emotional changes. As the world continues its wild ride, changes come at us faster and harder. Still dropping housing values and foreclosures, difficulty in gaining credit, corporate and personal bankruptcies, job losses and underemployment. Global warming. Seemingly random acts of nature that kill tens of thousands of people. Warring factions within and across countries and families. Children born. Breakthroughs discovered. Families built. Beautiful works of art created. Communities coming together to produce greatness. We need to work at embracing these changes and using them to head to the place where we want to be.

This story is of a significant personal transition for our teenaged son. His summer fun of playing three sports and spending lazy afternoons was over. He was starting classes at a new high school. It is a school in a different town. He knew maybe a half dozen kids in this new school. He left all of the kids he has known since kindergarten.

Whether it is a change we want or a change we don't, William Bridges says there are three steps to a change: the ending, the neutral zone, and the new beginning.[1] The ending is of what was, of what could have been, of what will not be. It is a realization. An understanding. We may not be ready for what will be. Yet we no longer have what was. In the "neutral zone", people go through a cycle with stages Elisabeth Kübler-Ross labeled as grief, including denial, anger, bargaining, depression, and

---

[1] Bridges, William (1991). *Managing Transitions: Making the Most of Change*. Reading, MA: Addison-Wesley Publishing Company.

acceptance. [2] It is only with acceptance that people are ready to go forward into the new beginning, to move on.

For our son, the transition began many months earlier, when we learned about the possibility of his going to this school. His transition followed the typical pattern. His first response was to be incredulous we would even suggest it. He was angry with our lack of parental understanding "no way, no how – I won't leave my friends; I've been looking forward to going to this other school for my whole life". He had trouble focusing (although that could just be typical teenager behavior). Once he learned a little more, he said "not likely, but I'm keeping an open mind". As parents, we give him a lot of credit for keeping an open mind at this point – it is more than many people several times his age are able to do. When he went to visit the school, it was "well, maybe", though he was still sad about moving on from his lifelong friends. After spending a day at the school, it was "most definitely". He moved into visioning the possibilities that might come to pass. He's been on a cloud ever since learning that he is truly going and has never looked back

---

[2] Kübler-Ross, Elizabeth (1969). *On Death & Dying*. Simon & Schuster/Touchstone.

to second guess his decision. To start out positively, we're hosting a party at our home so he can get to know his new classmates and the families can meet each other.

In our lives, there are so many transitions happening that it is hard to keep count. Especially in crazy times. Change is truly our constant. Our old mental reality that may have been rooted in stability ends and we move into the chaos of the neutral zone. Getting to your personal new beginning will take a lot of work.

What transitions are you going through right now? Perhaps you are between relationships. Perhaps your current relationships are in crisis. Perhaps you are between jobs. Perhaps you still have your job but see the proverbial writing on the wall that your position may be going away. Perhaps your job is secure, but it is not something that helps you get to that place where you want to be.

What is hard in a time of transition is believing the transition presents exactly the opportunity you need to move closer to that place where you want to be. A risk for all of us, especially when we experience what we consider to be bad results, is to self reproach, to mentally beat ourselves up for being in this situation – whatever the personal "this" may be. Yet, doing this adds no value. The past is in your rearview mirror. No matter how much time you spend obsessing, there is no do-over button you can push to change the past.

Reflecting on the Theodore Roosevelt quote at the start of this chapter, so maybe you did not get the ultimate result you hoped. Okay. Move on. It is far better to have at least tried something and failed than lay on your deathbed wishing for you could have tried something and didn't. And so now, try again. Turn the page. Begin work on the next assignment.

Since you're still living, you're in transition. To help this along, make a list of what is ending for you. Maybe it is a job. Perhaps it is a shift in financial position. Maybe nothing has actually changed, yet some thing is causing anxiety – resulting in your feeling like even good happenings are nothing more than bright paint covering rotted wood. Consider the positive and negative aspects of the change. Depending on where your head and heart are, you may only be able to see the negative possibilities. Stretch yourself and see where previously unsuspected possibilities may lie.

Now think about where you are in the grief cycle of denial, anger, bargaining, depression, and acceptance. Why? What will it take to help you move forward?

Next, consider the future after this transition. What are the possibilities that you may not have been open to seeing because you were in a comfortable place? Which two will help you get to the place where you want to be?

My personal action plan

What is ending for me? _____

_____

_____

_____

_____

_____

What are positive and negative aspects about what is

ending? _____

_____

_____

_____

Where am I in the grief cycle: denial, anger, bargaining,

depression, and acceptance? _____

Why?_____

_____

_____

_____

What is keeping me here, at this stage?_____

_____

_____

_____

Opportunities to explore to get to the place where I want to be:

1._____

_____

2._____

_____

My specific next steps:

_____

_____

_____

_____

_____

_____

_____

_____

_____

_____

_____

_____

_____

Today's Date_____

Date I Will Check Back In _____

Being accountable to myself

Where am I in the grief cycle now? _____

How have new circumstances affected this? _____

_____

_____

_____

What are the opportunities in what I am experiencing?

_____

_____

_____

Where do I see hope? _____

_____

_____

How can I help bring hope to someone else? _____

_____

_____

What is my next step?_____

_____

_____

_____

_____

Date_____

Never make predictions, especially about the future. –
Casey Stengel, Baseball player & manager (1891 –
1975)

When your crystal ball is clear as mud

The story

The future is as clear as mud. We may have ideas,
hopes, wants and wishes, but we don't really know for
sure what will happen in the future. As this is written, the
world economy is going through an economic crisis.
Pundit predictions of double digit US unemployment have
come true. Such predictions were considered outlandish
only a few months ago. Foreclosures are up. Portfolios
are down. The price of oil swings like the mood of a
hormonal teen.

So how do we deal? How do we cope? One skill that
can help us successfully through tough times is the ability
to handle situations that are unclear. We need to make
sure we are able to deal with ambiguity.

The tough thing is that we want two plus two to equal four. Yet, life is messy. With things as clear as mud, two plus two could equal four or twenty seven or umbrella or dolphin or hop on one foot or nothing or infinity. Our standard structured approaches may not serve us well. Solutions may not be easily seen. Outcomes may be anything but certain.

So what is your choice? Do you throttle back on risk? Look for the safest way? Just do what you've always done? Bend over backwards to make sure mistakes are not made? Some level of conservatism may be the right thing to do. But if all you do is batten down the hatches, you will certainly block yourself from opportunities that come from the current chaos.

What is happening in your business? In your home? In your head? Some say it is best to avoid sticking your neck out for fear your head will be cut off. However, the business outlook is also clear as mud. Failing to innovate could result in failure. Seemingly safe, risk-avoiding behavior could cause you to be a contributing factor to the demise of everything from your business to your relationships.

A person who is skilled in dealing with unclear situations is able to comfortably handle risk and uncertainty. This has three elements. The first is to know what is your intent. To know the place where you want to be. Whether you will get there or not is not guaranteed. But if you shoot for the stars and only hit the moon, you are still much further along than when you started.

The second element is to acknowledge that the situation is unclear. Accept where you are and what is happening. Ask questions. Understand the past. Know the outcome is uncertain, that there is really no sure thing, that every action with risk of success also has risk of failure.

The third element is to actually deal with the situation. Yes, take action. Focus on what you can control. Break what needs to be done into manageable parts and take it on one piece at a time. Do your best. Decide. Act. Will it be perfect? Probably not. Prepare to forgive yourself for what did not go as well as you wish it had. Will there be people who find fault with what you did? Absolutely. Embrace their feedback as a gift and a way to make you better the next time.

My assignment

This assignment for dealing with situations that are as clear as mud is a more of/less of exercise. First, observe the habits of people who seem to handle ambiguity well. Consider which traits/trends you can emulate. Watch how they focus, decide and act, build their resilience, keep composure.

Next, consider how this could be applied to you. Prioritize your top two action items and do more of them. Only two. Seriously. Sometimes we overwhelm ourselves by trying to focus on too many things at the same time.

Here's what you need to do less of: obsessing over the path not taken; seeking 100% answers; getting defensive in the face of feedback—if you don't get at least a little pushback, perhaps you are not pushing far enough. Finally, one more "do less of" item: shut down the things that sap your energy. For some people, it is the 24/7 bombardment of the news. The world will not end if you turn off CNN or Fox News for a while and take a walk outside.

My personal action plan

This is a person who seems to do a decent job of dealing with ambiguity:_____

This is what I see him/her do to handle ambiguity, to build resilience, and to retain composure: _____

_____

_____

_____

_____

_____

_____

_____

_____

_____

_____

_____

_____

_____

_____

_____

Here are two things I can learn from this person and apply to my situation to better handle ambiguity:

1._____

_____

2._____

_____

Here is my action plan to do these two things:

_____

_____

_____

_____

_____

This is one thing I am going to do less of: _____

_____

_____

This is how I am going to implement it: _____

_____

_____

Today's Date_____

Date I Will Check Back In _____

Being accountable to myself

From the person who handles ambiguity well, what one lesson did I apply to my own situation? _____
_____
_____

What was my response to the more of/less of exercise?
_____
_____
_____

What am I proud of? _____
_____
_____

What would make it even better? _____
_____
_____

What is my next step?_____
_____
_____
_____
_____
_____

Date_____

If each of us were to do what we are capable of doing, we would absolutely astound ourselves. – Thomas Alva Edison, Inventor (1847 – 1931)

Do what makes you sparkle

The story

What is it that you absolutely LOVE to do? You know, that thing that just revs your engine? The thing that makes you sparkle inside and out. What is it?

For my son, the world revolves around baseball. Since he was big enough to hold a bat, baseball has been his thing. His first few seasons he would sleep with a mitt under his pillow, just to be closer to the game. Sure, he enjoys school, football, basketball, tennis, his friends, the dog, video games, pizza, and – most the time – his sister. But when it comes to what revs his engine, it is baseball. It puts a spring in his step and a gleam in his eye.

Between playing and umpiring, he does something with baseball most days between the time the robins appear in the spring and the end of the school year. With every new season, there is a fresh optimism. He tells everyone "we will be a GREAT team this year – I think we can win it all". Astounding us with anti-teenage behavior, he even gets up early on Saturday to practice – dressed and ready to go even before his wake-up alarm sounds.

At the other end of the spectrum, this message is written a month since the end of the swimming season. Swimming is my daughter's thing. She is Queen Chlorine. During a typical week, she'll swim four to six days and still be the last one out of the pool after practice. While she plays basketball and volleyball in the off season, she counts down the weeks before the start of the next swim season. During the off season, we can see that there is clearly something missing for her. Her sparkle is a little less bright.

Let's apply these lessons to ourselves. If we want to physically, mentally, emotionally and financially live in the place where we want to be, what does it look like? Is it focused on people? Education? Helping children?

Feeding the hungry? Helping the homeless? Saving animals? Is it in building and perfecting processes? Developing or using technology? Creating and innovating? Implementing the work of others? What will signal to you that you are there?

In talking with senior citizens with memories of the Great Depression – or who were raised by Depression era parents – something that comes out loud and clear is that those times of hardship were the good old days. In hindsight, they see where they were able to find internal fortitude they didn't know they had. They built lasting friendships based on shared struggle rather than mirrored pretense and posturing. A common refrain is that they didn't know how good they had it until it was long past.

What does this mean for you today? It would be a shame to look in the rear view mirror of your life many years from now and see that you missed out on appreciating your own "good old days" while you were in them. The only thing promised to you for sure is today. So today, right now, choose to work on becoming your best. Get yourself to that place where you want to be. Do what makes your sparkle bright. Let yourself shine..

This assignment is to consider how you are when you are in that season when you sparkle? Are you there now? If so, stretch further and astound yourself.

Has your sparkle dimmed? Are you between seasons and not living your passion?   Have you forgotten what it is? Are you wondering whether you ever had one? Now is the time to look at what it will take to get to the place where you want to be.

List things that gave you purpose in the past. What are possibilities now? What will it take to get you there? Highlight the things in your control to get your sparkle.

Your challenge is to look at your current situation. What elements of what you have today make you sparkle? How does this relate to what may be your greater purpose, your ability to be your best? How can you leverage what is in your present, your reality today, to fulfill your purpose, to get you to the place where you want to be?

My personal action plan

What has given me purpose in the past?_____

_____

_____

_____

_____

What do I see as my purpose now? _____

_____

_____

_____

_____

What are the common elements of these things?

Financial._____

_____

Mental._____

_____

Physical._____

_____

Emotional. _____

_____

Spiritual. _____

_____

What are possibilities for me to sparkle within my present circumstances? _____

_____

_____

_____

_____

_____

What is in my control? _____

_____

_____

_____

_____

What are my personal next steps? _____

_____

_____

_____

_____

_____

_____

Today's Date_____

Date I Will Check Back In _____

Being accountable to myself

How's Operation Sparkle going? Which of my action
steps have I accomplished? _____

_____

_____

What's my next step to achieving my action plan?

_____

_____

_____

_____

What can I do to help someone else restore their
sparkle? _____

_____

_____

_____

_____

_____

Date_____

Act

PART IV. Act: moving forward to implement your decisions

In the action phase you are making choices to create the masterpiece that is you. You are taking the action to get to the place where you want to be, to fulfill your mighty purpose. By the time you get to this set of choices, you already clarified your mighty purpose, the place where you want to be. You already worked through the grief of your crazy time and accepted yourself and your situation. You already explored opportunities and decided which ones to purse and which ones to leave behind. Now it is time to move forward, to act.

Depending on the craziness of your situation, the time to work through an action plan may need to be shorter or longer. The important thing to do now is define your action plan, break it into achievable parts, and actually do something. In this way, you are creating that work of art that is you. You are moving forward to get yourself to that place where you want to be. You are taking yourself to your personal place of contentment and gratitude and mighty purpose. To where you feel sane. To where you appreciate what you are and what you are contributing to your piece of the world. To having a mindset of what you need to do to make a fair number of healthy choices and remember to smile in appreciation.

When you take action, this means you move on. No more just talking about it. No more thinking, plotting, and scheming. This is when you do. No excuses. No sense of victimness. No apologies. If you find you need to revise the place where you want to be, okay, so be it. Course correct. Go back to the messages in Part I – Clarify. But if you are ready to move on, do it. Act.

We can't solve problems with the same thinking that created them. – Albert Einstein, Physicist & Nobel Prize winner (1879 – 1955)

Getting unstuck from the tar

The story

Ever get yourself into trouble? Of course you have. We all have. We all will again. We get ourselves in trouble by what we do and by what we fail to do. What we say and what we fail to say. Our choices get us into trouble. Our choices can also get us out of trouble.

What often happens, though, is we get into a situation and then we get stuck. It feels like we stepped into soft tar – it just grabs us and keeps us from moving forward to where we want to go. Maybe we don't know what to do next. Maybe we know what needs to be done next but don't know how to do it. Maybe we are afraid of failure. Maybe we are afraid of success.

When in crazy times, people often experience a loss of energy. They feel worn out. Tired. There are things they want to do. They just can't figure out how to get to them. So maybe they dawdle. Or nap. Or hang out with cyber-friends on FaceBook. Or zone out in front of the TV. Or. Or. Or. The ways to self-distract are probably infinite. At the end of the day, they haven't gotten any further along in what they are trying to do, so they beat themselves up for not getting it done.

One personal "stuck in the tar" area for me was in starting this book series. So many people encouraged me that I finally decided to do it. But there was a long distance between decision and action. Years, actually.

A couple times I did get unstuck only to get myself stuck again. Then you should have seen how the excuses piled up! Okay, it was a combination of excuses and blaming. In what should surprise no one, most of the blaming pointed at others, not where it belonged: with me. It all had to do with things outside of my control. I engaged in a mental game of blaming and self-victimization that could be made into a screenplay. Here are a couple scenes:

- I was not able to finish the book because I was too busy being a good mom and wife.
- I was not able to finish the book because my employer was in bankruptcy and I had anxiety over my job.
- I was not able to finish the book because it was summer time and there were other things to do.
- I was not able to finish the book because because because.

By the time this first book was finished, it was longer than the gestation time for both of my children!

In truth, I was hiding from myself and my fear of what could be next, when I was no longer "working on the book." What if the book sold and it took me away from life as I knew it? What if the book didn't sell and I was a failure? What if nothing changed? I was stuck in mental tar of my own making, afraid of my own made up "what if" world of negativity.

One thing I love about the Einstein quote at the start of this message is what it does NOT say. Please note: he focuses on the thinking we used before. He does NOT say that we cannot use the same people. What he says is just that we need to shift our thinking. What this means is we truly do have the ability to get out of where we are now and move closer to the place where we want to be. We truly do have the capability to move forward to our mighty purpose. Although that journey of a thousand miles begins with a single step, that first step is a big one. If we want to get to that place where we want to be, we need to choose to take that first step. And then do it.

To get beyond being stuck in the mental tar with this book, I needed to stop hiding and victimizing myself. I needed to change my thinking. I needed to take look at what I could control and then take a breath and let go of things I could not control. I needed to get my support systems in place. Then I needed to sit down, focus and do the necessary hard work.

So now, what about you? Where are you stuck in the mental tar today? Where are you far away from the place where you want to be, from fulfilling your mighty purpose? Where are you making yourself into a victim? Where are you mentally bullying yourself? Kind of a harsh concept isn't it? Yet, it is precisely what we do when we choose to cope by hiding from the need to take action.

You can absolutely choose to make today the day you escape the mental tar. You can absolutely choose to move beyond the thinking that keeps you from your purpose. You can absolutely choose to move beyond your "what if" into action. You can absolutely choose to try. Do it today.

My assignment

This assignment is to get out of the mental tar holding you back from the place where you want to be. Today is the day to try. Today is your day to jump into action.

Start now. You have already been evaluating your possibilities. You know the pros and cons of so many potential next steps. While you don't know for certain whether you will be successful, you do know for certain that you will not be successful if you do not try. You will not move closer to the place where you want to be if take no action.

Choose to start now. What is one thing you will put in place today?

My personal action plan

This is where I am stuck in the mental tar: _____

_____

_____

_____

These are the excuses/rationalization/justifications I use
to keep myself in the tar: _____

_____

_____

These are the possible things I could choose to do to get
unstuck._____

_____

_____

_____

_____

_____

_____

_____

This is the one thing I will do today to get unstuck.

1._____

_____

_____

_____

This is my next step toward getting unstuck: _____

_____

_____

_____

_____

_____

_____

_____

This is my plan to do it (date):_____

_____

_____

_____

_____

_____

_____

_____

_____(_____)

Now put the book down and go do it. Really.

No kidding. No whining. Take control. Go already.

Today's Date_____

Date I Will Check Back In _____

158

Being accountable to myself

How did doing the one thing work out? _____
_____
_____
What went well? _____
_____
_____
What could have gone better? _____
_____
_____
What will I do differently next time? _____
_____
_____
Based on what I know now, what is my next one thing to do (date)? _____
_____
_____
_____
_____(_____)

Go make it happen.

Date_____

Failing to plan is planning to fail. – Alan Lakein,
Personal time management expert

Pack your bags & go

My husband is a wonderful planner. Me? Not so
much. He is the one with the very thorough records. He
has systems in place for darn near everything. While he
was not a boy scout, he has wonderful scouting practices
and is always prepared.

When we take a trip that is overnight or longer, he
prints out a checklist he has developed over the years.
For the sake of nostalgia he keeps on the list the sleepy
friends (stuffed animals) that our kids always brought
along to snuggle with at bedtime. There is a listing of
special items for baseball tournaments, a listing of
special items for swim meets, and a listing of items for
camping trips.

I used to tease him about this list. Note the "used to." After all, I was a seasoned business traveler who was experienced in hitting three continents in a single trip. Tossing scorn at my in-laws who would start packing for a trip a month before it occurred, I would typically throw my stuff in a suitcase the morning I was to leave. After all, I was a seasoned business traveler (did I mention that?).

Then I took a business trip to a conference at Disney World. The most magical place on earth. This was one of those trips where I took a shuttle from the airport to the conference center and was basically a prisoner on the Disney campus until the return shuttle took me to the airport to go back home. Upon arriving, I took a shower to clean up from the trip and prepare for afternoon meetings. In the suitcase I packed a couple hours before, I found shirts and skirts, shoes and stockings. But one important type of garment was missing. No underwear. Oops.

Fortunately for me, the conference center had souvenir shops aplenty. There was precisely one selection available in ladies' underwear. It was a tri-pack with each pair covered in little patterns of Winnie-the-

Pooh, Tigger, or Eeyore. Thanks to the Disney character underwear, I had a little bit of an extra fun attitude throughout that conference, to be sure. And for years to follow, I had a reminder of the importance of properly packing my bags every time I opened my lingerie drawer and saw Tigger smiling up at me.

So what did I learn? My husband will say the first lesson is to revere him and not mercilessly mock his packing list. Hopefully I learned this at least a little bit. I am much more diligent in going through the checklist. We encourage our kids to do this as well. What I also learned is that while it is easy to overlook something you may need to bring along on your journey, the error is probably not fatal. There will be times where there is something you need that you don't have. Usually there are ways to figure out how to make due.

How does this apply to getting to being your best, to the place where you want to be? Let's say you went through the loss process. You evaluated your opportunities. Now you're ready to act. Ready to fulfill your purpose. Wonderful. Get ready to pack your bags and go.

But wait. As you get ready to go, there is a bit more planning to do. You need to plan for what you will need for the trip to being your best, to fulfilling your mighty purpose. As you prepare, consider:

- How will you get there?
- What resources will you need along the way?
- What will you want to do once you get there?
- How will you know when it is time to leave?
- What could possibly go wrong?

By thinking through possible what-ifs at the outset, you will be ready if and when they happen. The virtue of doing the planning is to improve your chances of success, not to cancel the trip. The tough thing in this, though, is the balance. Reality is that there are some things that are in our control. Reality is also that there are some things that are not in our control. We can spend our lifetimes worrying about the things not in our control and miss the beauty of today. Sometimes it is in being open to the detours that make our adventure even richer. And if the worst thing that happens is you end up with Tigger underwear, then you're probably doing okay.

So now make your checklist, pack your bags and go.

My assignment

When on your way to being your best, here are some questions you may want to consider to enhance your readiness:

- What do you want to do?
- Why? What is the benefit of doing it? What is the risk of not doing it?
- What are your concerns and risks if you do it?
- Of these concerns and risks, what are the things you cannot control?
- How can you eliminate or minimize the risks in your control?

My personal action plan

I want to do this: _____

_____

_____

_____

_____

Why I want to do it: _____

_____

_____

_____

_____

_____

_____

My concerns and risks: _____

_____

_____

_____

_____

_____

_____

The things I cannot control: _____

_____

_____

_____

_____

_____

_____

_____

How to minimize the risks I can control: _____

_____

_____

_____

_____

_____

_____

_____

_____

Today's Date_____

Date I Will Check Back In _____

Being accountable to myself

What are my learning as I prepare to pack my bags and go?_____

_____

_____

Which of my risks and concerns actually occurred?

_____

_____

_____

How did I handle it when they happened? _____

_____

_____

_____

Where did I over prepare? _____

_____

_____

What am I doing to be ready for what may come next?

_____

_____

_____

_____

Date_____

Be like a duck. Calm on the surface, but always paddling like the dickens underneath. – Michael Caine – Actor (1933 –)

Keep calm and carry on

The story

Recently, a friend sent me a poster with these words: Keep Calm and Carry On. The phrase comes from a series of posters commissioned by the British government over 70 years ago to help citizens stay positive in times of crisis. Thanks to a combination of a good message and the viral power of the web, poster replicas are showing up on everything from t-shirts to rugs. The message was even the title of a February 2009 article in *The Economist*.

In our home, we've framed the poster and hung it so it can be seen from our dinner table and the area our kids do homework.   It is our constant reminder. While any of us can choose to go from zero to 60 on the emotional scale in a nanosecond, the poster reminds us we can also choose to keep calm and carry on. It means that we can choose to ask and listen. We can choose to understand first and talk second. We can choose to continue to work toward our purpose.

Crazy times present us with interesting choices. What we probably already know is how the craziness is manifesting in our lives. Perhaps it is lack of income. Perhaps it is lack of sleep. Perhaps it is distance from loved ones or brokenness in our relationships.

What we choose now defines us. This is not the time to choose to panic or run away from work that needs to be done. It is not the time to choose to freeze up. It is not the time to choose to hide from reality or sugar-coat the truth. Now is the time to move forward with purpose. To keep stretching. To treat each other and ourselves with dignity. To make good choices. To be compassionate. To build and maintain resilience. To be kind to each other. To be grateful. To remember to smile.

Now is a perfect time to consider how to keep your mind calm and your actions purposeful. Even though times may be crazy, now is a perfect time to remember to express appreciation. Finally, now is also a perfect time to look out as well as in by helping someone else. Keep calm and carry on.

This assignment is to look at and in yourself. Where do things feel out of control? Are there themes? Sometimes we feel out of control in every area of our life. Sometimes, it is more localized, such as with some relationships and not others. Sometimes things are great at home and not at work. Or vice-versa. Sometimes life can be so overwhelming that the out of control feeling in one area spills over into other areas.

What are you doing to keep calm and carry on? Is doing these things easy or hard? Why? Where you are doing well? What can you carry into other areas?

With regard to others in your life, consider this: how can you help someone else to keep calm and carry on?

My personal action plan

Where am I feeling out of control? _____

_____

_____

_____

_____

What are the common themes for when I am feeling out
of control? _____

_____

_____

_____

_____

_____

What am I doing to keep calm and carry on? _____

_____

_____

_____

_____

_____

_____

Which things are easier? Which are harder?

Easier:_____

_____

Harder:_____

_____

What can I carry forward to bring calm into other areas of my life? _____

_____

_____

_____

_____

_____

_____

What can I do to help someone else keep calm and carry on?_____

_____

_____

_____

_____

_____

_____

Today's Date_____

Date I Will Check Back In _____

Being accountable to myself

How am I choosing to keep calm and carry on? Here is a list of what I can celebrate having done well: _____

_____

_____

_____

Where am I feeling frazzled? _____

_____

_____

What is my next step to transfer my successes to the currently frazzled areas? _____

_____

_____

Where am I seeking help? _____

_____

Where am I offering help?_____

_____

What's my next step?_____

_____

_____

_____

Date_____

The ultimate measure of a man is not where he stands in moments of comfort and convenience, but where he stands at times of challenge and controversy. – Martin Luther King, Jr., Minister & civil rights activist (1929 – 1968).

When we trip along the way

The story

Sometimes, we trip along the path on the way to the place where we want to be. Sometimes it is because of something we do. Sometimes it is because of something someone else does. Sometimes it is due to an act of nature. Sometimes there is no plausible explanation of why. When adversity comes along the path to where we want to be, this is when our resolve is tested. This is when our character is built. This is definitely when we need to retain our focus and keep our calm.

When we are tested along the way, it would be easy to slip into victim mode. Yet doing this helps no one, especially oneself. A lesson learned from a young friend may be instructive.

The place where my friend wanted to be was on the top level tennis team for his school. It was a long term goal and he worked extremely hard to get there. In fact, for the prior year and a half, he was a teen possessed. Every chance he had, he played tennis. He rushed to finish his schoolwork so he could play. He'd cajole drivers in his family to brave snowy roads so he could go practice. When he had no one to play against him, he would hit against a wall or with a machine to serve to him.

No kidding, this kid's passion was astounding. His enthusiasm was engaging. At the end of the summer, it was time for tryouts. He went into them ready. Primed and pumped. Well rested and well fed.

As we all held our collective breath waiting for the outcome, it was with a wink and a smile. No doubt about it. This kid had worked so hard that he was certainly going to make the team. Celebration preparations were being made in the background.

Collectively, we were all wrong. He did not earn a place on the team he wanted. He was given a spot on what was a lesser team. While he had a place to play for the season, it clearly was not the place where he wanted to be.

That he did not make the desired team was both a disappointment and an opportunity. This kid really worked his tail off. He learned to work hard. He learned to prioritize. He felt the energy and joy that comes with following passion. On these bases alone, he was a success.

Consider, though, did he also fail because he did not make the team? On one level, the level that looks to whether he got what he wanted, I guess we could say "yes, he failed." But if we abandon the analysis at this point, then we also fail.

Reality is that sometimes we do not get what we want on our own timetable. It could be that while we think we are ready for what we want, maybe we aren't yet. It could be that the thing we want is not yet ready for us.

Consider when you have learned your biggest life lessons, the lessons that shape your character. If you are like most people, the biggest lessons were when you worked through adversity. When I look at the things that have shaped my character and some of the best things in my life, it was invariably due to dealing with something I did not want. A class I had to take. A job assignment I really did not want to have. A place I did not want to live. But for these things ....

My friend's test is indicative of how he will develop as an adult. At first, we were not sure whether he would take this defeat as an opportunity. We were hoping he would consider what else he could do physically and emotionally to complement his tennis play: his diet, his sleep patterns, his flexibility, his mental state when he plays. We wondered if he would quit the team because he was not placed where he wanted to be placed. It certainly was a possibility. We were afraid he would become a kid who only plays tennis on his Wii. More importantly, we knew that the choices he would make during the storm of emotion would set the pattern for how he handles adversity for his lifetime.

Yes, he did stomp around and get angry and hurt and upset for a while, within the privacy of his home. I must say that I've been known to do this in times of defeat as well. I will bet you have, too. But we don't have to just suck it up and accept defeat. The passion and energy we put into trying to obtain what we did not, at this juncture needs to go inward or outward, so it is better to find a healthy outlet and let it out rather than to let it burn inside or be spent through unhealthy choices.

After his hurt and anger were spent, he had other choices to make. What he wisely chose was to stay calm, to lift his head up, to put his shoulders back, to look this lesson in the eye and to grow strong. As this is written, the tennis season is coming to a close. The season-end report is that my friend chose to work hard as a fully participating member of the (lesser) team on which he was placed. He chose to have a good attitude and be a positive member of the team. He worked hard and excelled. He did so well that he was able to play in an "invitation only" event and win some matches.

I could not be more proud of this young man. Not that I wanted him to be kept from the thing that he wanted. To the contrary, I wanted it for him wholeheartedly. But if it wasn't meant to be at this time, then what I wanted for him was to learn well and develop as a man of strong character. Years from now he may see not making the other team as one of the best things that ever happened to him.

And so it is for us. To paraphrase the Martin Luther King, Jr. quote at the beginning of this chapter, it is not our response to the easy times that is the measure of who we are. It is our response when we are challenged.

When we are on our way to the place where we want to be, we have to expect obstacles and plan accordingly. We also need to be aware that unexpected or unforeseeable obstacles can and will occur. Those are our times of opportunity, our times to step it up, our times to stay in the game, our times when our resolve is tested.

What is your choice? Do you choose to get mad and pout and blame and be a victim? Or do you choose to stay focused, resolve to move from disappointment to learning, re-decide among the opportunities, and then act in a way to move forward?

My assignment

This assignment is to help you be ready for when you trip along the way to the place where you want to be.

Start by considering your disappointments to see how they have resulted in some of the best things that make you the person you are. Consider your steps from disappointment to learning. Was there a point where you chose to rise from having a victim mentality to choosing to be personally accountable for your next steps? Is there something in this that you can use to help yourself or someone else when they are dealing with a difficult time?

Most likely, when you look back, you will also see you had responses that you would like to not repeat the next time. Where you sabotaged your own best interests. What is it you would like to do differently the next time? What can you do to make sure you make better, more positive choices?

If you are tripping now, how are you applying more positive choices?

My personal action plan

This is where I have been disappointed in the past: _____

_____

_____

_____

This is where some of my disappointments resulted in
good things: _____

_____

_____

This is what happened along my path from
disappointment to learning to growth:_____

_____

_____

If I chose to initially allow myself to be a victim of the
situation, this was my turning point to where I stopped
being a victim and chose to be personally accountable for
my next steps: _____

_____

_____

What learning from this can I use to help myself or
someone else when there is a trip on the path to the
place where I/they want to be: _____

_____

_____

This is where I have chosen to respond in ways I would prefer to not repeat: _____

_____

What have I done to sabotage my own best interests:

_____

_____

This is what I would like to do to make different, more positive choices the next time I trip along the way:_____

_____

_____

This is where I am presently tripping along the way: _____

_____

_____

_____

This is what I am going to do differently to make more positive choices:_____

_____

_____

_____

_____

_____

_____

Today's Date_____

Date I Will Check Back In _____

Being accountable to myself

After time and reflection, where am I tripping today?

_____

_____

This is how I am responding positively: _____

_____

_____

This is where I am still allowing myself to be a victim or struggling to respond in a way that I feel is honorable:

_____

_____

_____

This is where I have helped others who were tripping:

_____

_____

This is what was effective and helpful: _____

_____

_____

These are my thoughts about my next steps to go through adversity with dignity and an attitude of learning:

_____

_____

_____

Date_____

Those people blessed with the most talent don't necessarily outperform everyone else. It's the people with follow-through who excel. – Mary Kay Ash, Founder of Mary Kay Cosmetics and philanthropist (1918 – 2001)

Beyond just getting the book

The story

Just before the holidays, I was enjoying lunch with some colleagues. Conversation turned to activities of our children. I talked about our then-12 year old swimmer, Queen Chlorine, whose favorite habitat is the swimming pool. At the table was another colleague who is also the parent of a competitive swimmer. We talked about upcoming swim meets, the girls' competitive goals, and how proud we are of them.

Two of our colleagues confessed that they did not know how to swim. They added that this was something they planned to learn how to do. They further reported that on many occasions they went so far as to "get the book" as they called it. This meant that several times they received the book of swim class schedules at their local pool. They even went so far as to mentally consider which days/times could work for them. And that is as far as it went – for years!

One part of the job in our organization is to partner with our clients to understand and fix job performance issues. This made people at the table curious as to what was in the way of the non-swimmers. The question turned to what was preventing them from taking the plunge – so to speak. After some relatively lame excuse making, it was time for the big admission. They were what got in their own way of learning to swim.

It was easier to do nothing than to do something. Inertia is a powerful force. This has been known since the 1600s when Sir Isaac Newton published his first law of motion saying an object at rest stays at rest unless acted upon by an external force.

This made me wonder – where is it that we are allowing inertia to keep us from accomplishing our dreams? Why is it that the place we want to be so often becomes that far away wish that never comes true?

Consider your dreams unachieved. Is it that trip for which the brochure is in the back of your desk? The time with family members you will get to some day? That degree for which the application is on your hard drive? That book to finish writing? The instrument you want to play? Cuisine you want to cook? Volunteering at the charitable organization that has such great purpose? Woodworking? Learning to dance? Speaking another language? Racing? Juggling?

So before you close this book, it is time to ask and to act. Where is your inertia keeping you from contributing more fully? What are your unconfronted obstacles? Do you need to be better organized? To be better at speaking up? What do you need to give your best? If you are in a leadership role either in your home or at your work, what is keeping your team members from more fully contributing, from being more engaged? Where is inertia stopping you?

Crazy times happen. They are part of life presented to us to help us grow along our journey. Quit using them as the excuse keeping you away from the place where you want to be. Choose to not let them keep you from your mighty purpose. Today is the day to not let crazy times keep you from your dreams.

If you have been working through the exercises in this book, you know where you want to be. You accept your losses and understand your fears. You realize the opportunities in front of you and choose to act. If what you need is a job, do not let double digit unemployment deter you. Remember that what you need is one job, not a thousand. Don't let yourself close this book for the last time without the final step. Take action. Follow through. Hold yourself accountable. Keep the place where you want to be in your head and in your heart. Then go do what you need to do to get there.

Before you put this book down, be your own champion of the place where you want to be. Pick one thing. Do it. And then get yourself out of the way of your success. Move beyond just having the book. Take the plunge. Jump in with both feet. Okay, at least put your toe in the water. Move from aspiration to action. Do it now. Make this the day you follow through.

This final assignment is to be the champion of the place where you want to be. One more time, write down what you define as the place where you want to be. You need to write it down, to have it concretely defined. That way you will know which way you are headed, when you are on the right path, and when you are there.

Now, review the prior chapters. Pick one thing you know to be important to getting you to the place where you want to be that you just haven't done yet.

Next, be honest with yourself about what is getting in the way and what is in your control. For the things in your control, break them into smaller written action steps and commit to doing them by a date you define. Make this the day you follow through.

My personal action plan

Description of my purpose/the place where I want to be:

_____
_____
_____
_____
_____
_____
_____
_____
_____

One previous assignment still undone: _____

_____
_____
_____
_____

What is in my way of completing this assignment?

_____
_____
_____
_____

What part of the undone assignment is in my control?

_____

_____

_____

_____

_____

_____

What are my specific manageable action steps to getting
on with the things in my control (with dates)? _____

_____

_____

_____

_____

_____

_____

_____

_____

_____

_____

_____

_____(_____)

Today's Date_____
Date I Will Check Back In _____

Being accountable to myself

Which of the assignments were easy for me? _____

_____

_____

_____

Where am I still having a hard time?_____

_____

_____

_____

Since none of us is equipped with a "do over" button,
what is it that I am doing to set myself up for long-term
success? _____

_____

_____

_____

What's next for me?_____

_____

_____

_____

_____

_____

_____

Date_____

You gain strength, courage and confidence by every experience by which you really stop to look fear in the face. You are able to say to yourself, "I lived through this horror. I can take the next thing that comes along." – Eleanor Roosevelt, United Nations diplomat & US first lady (1884 – 1962)

Parting thoughts

May you go confidently in the direction of your dreams, to the place where you want to be, to where you fulfill your mighty purpose. For more information, look to

www.stayingsaneincrazytimes.com

or join in the conversation at:

http://stayingsaneincrazytimes.wordpress.com/

Thank you!

Acknowledgements

My sincere thanks to the many people who helped make this book possible. For my family, colleagues, and friends, I am deeply appreciative for your encouragement and support as what started as weekly messages sharing comments from known thought leaders morphed into sharing our wins and losses and successes and misadventures. For readers of my message series, thank you for both encouraging me to put these messages into book form and for forwarding the messages to your own families, colleagues, and friends.

To my clients, colleagues, bosses and friends who are or were with General Motors, a special thank you. You gave me the freedom to use my voice to encourage others to stay strong during one of the darkest times in General Motors' history.

To my professors and co-learners at Capella University, it was through your stretching my thinking that these messages even began. Special thanks to my extended dissertation team: April Boyington-Wall, Bill Reed, Gene Dixon, Ira Chaleff, JJ Klaver, Dennis Darlak, and Drew Detamore.

So many of my loved ones inspired the stories in this book. Wow do I appreciate how you share your lives and keep your sense of humor when I write about your adventures and misadventures, joys and sorrows. First and foremost, thank you to my husband, Brian, and our children, Zachary and Alyson. Your good-natured support in everything from story ideas, to editing, to putting up with my talking like a fortune cookie cannot be measured. Your loving ability to make every day with you even sweeter than the last is appreciated more than words can say.

Warm thanks to my parents, Jerry and Carol Orlaske, who keep score of which of them has been written about the most (this mention counts as one for each of you); to my sister Cynthia Orlaske-Ray and her husband Curtis Ray; to my brother Rob Orlaske and his late wife Heidi; and to generations of the Liberman and Krystal families. Thank you for the love and support.

And then to my friends. You helped me in ways large and small and probably in some ways I haven't even figured out yet. Special thanks to our neighbors, especially my dear walking partner-CPA-therapist Michele Scharg & family, Vivian Honig & family, Jill Bamford & family, and Pam Christian & family. Thank you Nancy Bates and Bill Dwyer for the gentle mentoring. Thank you Reyes, Wahler, and Weil families. And special thanks to our Orchard Grove Community Church family for the inspiration, love and support.

Much appreciation also goes to my artistic team. Joe Borri used his many creative gifts to convert what was not much of an idea into a cover I just love. Darrell Irwin of Vivid Light Photography creatively used shadow, light, and humor to make me sparkle for my author photo. Thank you both.

Finally, to you, the reader of this book, I am honored that you chose to gift me with your time and trust. Let's keep our conversation going. You can reach me at trich@richcounsel.com .

About the author

Theresa Rich, Ph.D. is an organization effectiveness consultant and attorney with a quarter century of business consulting experience with a Fortune 5 company and a decade of pro bono consulting in her community. She helped business leaders in over 20 countries to be more effective both as individuals and as teams.

Her upbeat, inspirational message series that triggered this book focuses on the theme of taking responsibility for our personal choices. These messages are virally circulated around the world to tens of thousands of people from all walks of life.

Theresa and her husband Brian Rich live in Farmington Hills, MI with Zachary and Alyson, their two wonderful children, and Kizmet the spoiled dog.

www.ingramcontent.com/pod-product-compliance
Lightning Source LLC
Chambersburg PA
CBHW070350090426
42733CB00009B/1353